BROKE ON MONDAY,

BOSS

BY FRIDAY

A 5-Day Structure To Build Your First Product Or Service

BY

ALEX GRAOROVSKI

Broke on Monday, Boss by Friday
Copyright © 2026 by Alex Graorovski

For permission requests or enquiries, contact:
info@brokeonmondaybossbyfriday.com

Disclaimer: The information presented in this book is a collection of advice and opinions. The author assumes no responsibility for any decisions, actions, or outcomes resulting from the use or implementation of the material contained herein. Some names, examples, and scenarios have been generalised or adapted to protect privacy while preserving the integrity of the concepts.

ISBN: 978-1-7645420-8-1

"Nothing changes until you enforce a point of no return."

TABLE OF CONTENTS

INTRODUCTION
THE WAKE-UP CALL TO TRANSFORMATION 1

DAY 1
BURN THE OLD, BUILD THE NEW................................. 10

DAY 2
WEAPONISE YOUR VALUE 25

Day 3
MAXIMUM VISIBILITY, MINIMUM TIME 37

DAY 4
SELL LIKE A BOSS.. 51

DAY 5
BOSS MODE – DELIVER, UPSELL & SCALE....................... 68

BONUS CHAPTERS
THE MARKETING BOSS PLAYBOOK 85
THE BOSS SALES PLAYBOOK 149

CONCLUSION
NO WAY BACK 237
COMMAND PAGE 241
100 BUSINESS IDEAS 243

ABOUT THE AUTHOR..244

THE 5-DAY STRUCTURE

WARNING

This book does not function as information. It removes the ability to claim confusion or uncertainty. Do not continue if you intend to read passively or preserve your current identity. Continuing beyond this page without execution is a deliberate act of self-betrayal.

INTRODUCTION
THE WAKE-UP CALL TO TRANSFORMATION

"Nobody is coming to save you. And that's the best news you'll ever hear."

That sentence hits with the truth, and you can't ignore it. Lost in the weight of your own thoughts. The familiar pull of uncertainty. The same job. The same routine. The same dream collecting dust in the back of your mind. That feeling "there has to be more" is not failure. It's potential, screaming to be used.

Every Boss starts there: Broke, uncertain, and tired of pretending mediocrity is normal.

THE REALITY CHECK

You don't lack talent. You lack clarity. Most people stay broke not because they can't earn more, but because they never define why they want more or how they'll create it.

They wait for permission. They confuse comfort with safety. They drown in information and starve for execution.

Boss Law #1: Excuses are just stories designed to protect comfort.

The world doesn't pay you for effort, it pays you for value delivered and problems solved. This book exists to collapse the gap between potential and proof.

FROM BROKE TO BOSS: THE SHIFT

A Boss isn't defined by wealth. A Boss is defined by command. Over time, their income, focus, and energy. To become one, you'll make three internal shifts:

1. From Victim → Architect
   Stop waiting for an opportunity. Design it.

2. From Consumer → Producer
   Stop scrolling for validation. Start creating solutions.

3. From Fear → Execution
   Stop thinking about what might go wrong. Move so fast that doubt can't catch up.

Boss Law #2: Confidence isn't a feeling; it's a result of consistent execution.

WHY YOU'RE HERE

If you picked up this book, something in you already snapped. You've been stuck, seen others move faster, live freer, and you're done watching from the sidelines. Good. Because the first step to power is disgust.

Disgust at your own hesitation. Disgust at wasted time. Disgust so deep it forces rebirth.

That fire? That's the same emotion that built every empire you've ever admired.

THE BOSS EQUATION

<u>Problem Finder + Solution Provider = Freedom</u>

This is the simplest business formula in the world, and the most ignored. You don't need to be a genius, influencer, or inventor. You just need to see problems others overlook and offer simple, valuable solutions fast. When you learn to think like this, money becomes a by-product of usefulness. You stop chasing cash and start creating value so real that people chase you.

THE POWER OF THE 5-DAY SYSTEM

This isn't just a book to read. It's a five-day holy grail designed to transform clarity into cash flow. Each day strips away another layer of limitation:

- Day 1: Burn the old identity, build the new.
- Day 2: Weaponise your value and turn skills into offers.
- Day 3: Build visibility with precision.
- Day 4: Sell with authority, not desperation.
- Day 5: Deliver, scale, and build your mini-empire.

By Friday, you'll have your first offer, your first audience, and a system you can run forever.

**Boss Law #3: Discipline is freedom
disguised as structure.**

HOW THIS BOOK WORKS

You'll move fast, reflect deeply, and execute daily. This book is built to be used.

Every chapter includes:
- Action Blueprints: precise step-by-step plans.
- Boss Laws: success principles condensed into one-liners.
- Perspective Breaks: moments that challenge how you think.
- Journal Prompts: short reflections to wire your mindset.

If you follow through, this week will compress years of trial and error into days of action.

WHY MOST PEOPLE QUIT

They expect results before consistency. They crave applause before mastery. They chase everything and commit to nothing. This book flips that script.

You'll learn the Straight-Line Method of momentum:
<u>clarity</u> → <u>commitment</u> → <u>cash</u> → <u>confidence</u>

Every small win compounds. Every action builds certainty. That certainty becomes momentum. And momentum is the secret currency of every Boss.

THE BOSS MINDSET

Being a Boss isn't about dominance; it's about ownership. Ownership of your thoughts, your time, and your outcomes. Every person who ever built something shared this trait: They accepted total responsibility for everything, even what wasn't their fault.

When you think like that, you take back control of your power. "A man who blames has handed over his future."

Stop blaming the algorithm, your job, your city, or your luck. You are the algorithm. You are the system. You are the variable that changes the result.

Boss Law #4: Results don't belong to the smartest;
they belong to the most certain.

REPROGRAMMING HOW YOU SEE VALUE

We've been conditioned to trade hours for dollars, not outcomes for freedom. That ends here. When you understand that value equals transformation, not time, you unlock leverage.

Leverage is how one person can out-earn a hundred employees. This book will teach you to identify, package, and deliver value so clearly that people can't ignore you.

THE POWER OF SPECIALISED KNOWLEDGE

The modern world doesn't reward generalists; it rewards specialists with leverage. Most people drown in information but never convert it into transformation. They know everything about nothing that pays them.

A Boss doesn't need to know everything. A Boss needs to know one thing deeply enough to solve real problems. That one skill, when refined, becomes your ticket out of survival mode.

Look at any leader you admire: They mastered one domain, then multiplied its value through clarity, packaging, and consistency.

You'll do the same with this book.
Your mind is your first business.
Your offer is the product of your discipline.

Boss Law #5: Specialised knowledge,
when combined with decisive execution,
becomes unstoppable leverage.

THE 3-PHASE VALUE LOOP

1. Discover: Identify what you know, what you can teach, or what you can solve.
2. Deliver: Package that skill into something people can buy.
3. Duplicate: Build systems so your value continues to work even when you don't.

Most people never reach phase 2. They get lost in perfection rather than in production. The following five days are your laboratory for speed. Proof through progress, not theory.

WHY THIS BOOK WORKS

Most courses fail because they rely on motivation instead of motion. You don't need hype, you need wins. This book uses the principle of momentum psychology: short, consecutive bursts of focused execution that rewire how you think, decide, and act.

- Day 1 resets identity.
- Day 2 weaponises value.
- Day 3 builds visibility.
- Day 4 master's persuasion.
- Day 5 creates scale.

Each day compounds, turning motion into mastery.

Boss Law #6: You don't rise to your goals,
you fall to your systems.

MOMENTUM OVER MOTIVATION

Motivation fades. Momentum compounds. You'll track visible progress daily, tiny victories that stack into confidence. Every time you take an action, even a small one, you tell your subconscious, "I'm the type who moves."

That identity becomes addictive. Within five days, your brain will crave action over hesitation. That's when transformation becomes permanent.

HOW TO USE THIS SYSTEM

This isn't a book to read once. It's a performance manual you revisit every time you level up. To get the most from it:

1. Commit to the schedule. Do one day at a time, no skipping ahead.
2. Print the checklists. Write things down; ink rewires belief faster than thought.
3. Do the journal prompts. They aren't optional, they're rewiring tools.
4. Finish every Action Blueprint. Half-completion equals zero transformation.
5. Re-run the challenge monthly. Each cycle deepens mastery.

By the end, you'll not only have your first client, product, or sale you'll have the clarity, structure, and confidence to repeat the process at will.

THE BOSS IDENTITY

A Boss doesn't chase validation. They create certainty.
A Boss doesn't beg for opportunity. They engineer it.
A Boss doesn't react. They design.

Once you see the world through this lens, you can't unsee it. Everything becomes a game of problem-solving and positioning. You realise money isn't scarce, clarity is. And clarity is built through decisions, not doubts. When you live by that rule, everything changes.

Boss Law #7: Every minute you waste
doubting yourself is a minute someone
else is monetising certainty.

FROM BROKE → BOSS: THE 5-DAY PROMISE

By the end, you'll:

- Know your profitable skill or offer.
- Have an irresistible value proposition people actually want.
- Understand how to build visibility without wasting time online.
- Sales systems that convert conversations into cash.
- And most importantly, carry the Boss Mindset that never settles for average.

This isn't theory. It's designed for proof.

Five days. Five breakthroughs. One permanent identity shift.

THE BOSS MANIFESTO

You started this book because you were tired of being stuck. By the time you finish it, you'll never look at work, money, or time the same way again. You'll stop asking, "Can I do this?" and start demanding, "How fast can I scale this?"

You'll learn that freedom isn't bought, it's built. One decision, one action, one day at a time. And when next Monday comes, you'll wake up differently. Not because the world changed, but because you did.

> Boss Law #8: There's no such thing
> as luck, only leverage created
> through relentless execution.

CALL TO ACTION

Read this book with urgency. Treat every page like a training ground. And understand this: You are not learning how to make money, you're learning how to command it.

By Friday, you won't just have an offer. You'll have an identity upgrade. The version of you that hesitated dies here.

Welcome to the new standard.

Welcome to Boss Mode.

DAY 1
BURN THE OLD, BUILD THE NEW

"To create a new future, you must first destroy the version of yourself that has kept you stuck in the past."

THE MONDAY RESET

It's Monday morning. The alarm hits 6 A.M. The heavy silence before your phone lights up with the same unpaid notifications, the same messages, the same loop. This is the moment where most people hit snooze, but not you, not anymore. Because deep down, you know this: You can't build a new life on the same identity that created the old one.

This isn't just another week. It's demolition day.
Identity Loop: <u>Old Beliefs</u> → <u>Old Actions</u> → <u>Old Results</u> → <u>Repeat</u>

Every transformation begins with a controlled burn.

You don't casually "improve" your life; you incinerate the patterns, excuses, and emotional addictions that keep you predictable.

THE CONTROLLED BURN PRINCIPLE

Fire doesn't just destroy, it purifies. When a forest burns, it releases seeds that germinate only in the heat of the flames. You're about to do the same for your identity.

Step 1: Expose the Dead Wood.
What habits, relationships, or beliefs no longer serve you?

Step 2: Set the Ignition Point.
Identify the one area where pain has turned to disgust. That's your energy source.

Step 3: Rebuild With Intention.
Once you've cleared the debris, rebuild only what aligns with your Boss Vision.

> Boss Law #9: Destruction without direction is chaos. Destruction with intention is creation.

THE THREE LIES THAT KEEP YOU BROKE

Every "broke" identity—financial, emotional, or professional—is built on three deeply ingrained lies. They're not just financial lies. They're neurological ones. They condition you to stay small.

Lie #1: "I Don't Have Time."

Time isn't a resource; it's a mirror. When you say you don't have time, what you really mean is "It's not a priority."

Reframe: High performers don't find time, they design it. Replace "I don't have time" with "I haven't made time yet." The difference is ownership.

Example Snapshot: A freelancer says they'll build their side income "when life calms down." Two years later, nothing's changed. Why? Because they're waiting for the world to organise around their weakness instead of structuring it around their mission.

Boss Law #10: If you don't schedule your priorities, life will schedule your distractions.

Time Ownership Model: <u>Reactive</u> → <u>Neutral</u> → <u>Proactive</u> → <u>Strategic</u>

Lie #2: "I Need Money to Make Money."

This one has killed more potential than failure ever could. It's the comfort blanket for inaction. The truth: You need courage, not capital.

Every empire started with one trade, value for trust. Not cash.

Real World Example: A creator starts with free value. Solving problems online, helping small clients, and building a reputation. The attention they earn becomes leverage. The leverage becomes revenue.

Principle: Money follows momentum, not intention.

Lie #3: "I'm Not Ready Yet."

This is perfectionism dressed as logic. Every "I'm not ready" hides the real fear: "I'm not enough." Here's the truth: Readiness is a result, not a requirement. Action creates readiness, experience builds confidence.

Micro Story: An entrepreneur delayed launching for six months to "refine their offer." Someone else launched a raw version in 48 hours, made their first $500, and refined from feedback. Six months later, the first person is still "preparing."

Boss Law #11: You'll never feel ready for
the life you were built to lead.

THE AFTERMATH OF LIES

Once you burn these three lies, something shifts. You stop negotiating with your potential and start dealing with reality.

No more "someday." Only strategy + execution.

Transition Moment. The Shift Begins: You've destroyed the false stories. Now we rebuild the truth. Welcome to the phase where you become what most people never dare to: a Creator.

THE CONSUMER → CREATOR SHIFT

You've burned the old. You've stripped away the excuses. Now it's time to build the new.

Most people think success starts with a strategy. It doesn't. It begins with identity: The moment you stop being a consumer of the world and become a creator of it.

The Attention Exchange Graph: Consumers trade time for entertainment. Creators trade value for attention, and attention becomes leverage.

A consumer waits for opportunities → A creator builds them.
A consumer scrolls for dopamine → A creator ships for data.
A consumer says, "One day." → A creator says, "Today."

Why Consumption Kills Confidence

Every scroll, binge, or "research session" feels productive, but it's a trap. When you absorb without creating, your brain confuses learning with doing. Confidence doesn't come from knowledge. It comes from momentum.

Boss Law #12: Creation builds confidence; consumption builds confusion.

That's why so many smart people stay broke. They know more than everyone, but they execute less than anyone.

4 C's Framework. From Passive to Productive
1. Clarity: Define what you stand for.
2. Consistency: Show up daily, even when it's ugly.
3. Courage: Publish before you feel ready.
4. Conversion: Turn value into trust, and trust into income.

Case Study: Turning Discipline into Opportunity

After stepping away from competitive sport, I discovered that the same principles that drive peak performance—discipline, consistency, and structured execution—are identical to those that build success in business.

Years of dedication had forged more than athletic ability; it had built a mindset of focus, repetition, and leadership. When I analysed that specialised knowledge and applied it to helping others, it became a business foundation.

I began sharing what I knew, structured training, high-performance habits, and practical mindset lessons. Nothing overproduced. No waiting for perfection. Just clear, consistent value.

Momentum followed naturally. The results created a reputation. Networking and experience multiplied opportunities.

"Discipline built the skill.
Consistency built trust.
Creation built the future."

The formula hasn't changed in sport or business: Show up, execute with intent, and keep building.

The 4 C's in Practice

Each "C" compound. Every post, call, or project is a vote for your new identity. That's how creators rise, not through viral luck but through repeated proof of consistency.

4 C's Model Flow Chart:
Idea → Action → Feedback → Iteration → Influence

Reprogramming Your Daily Inputs

To become a creator, your environment must change before your results do.

- Audit your feed.
  Unfollow anyone who makes you feel like you're behind. Follow those who teach you something valuable.

- Shift from entertainment to execution.
  For every hour you consume, you owe yourself an hour of creation.

- Replace reaction with documentation.
  Instead of watching someone else's success story, start recording yours—even if it's rough.

*Quote Callout: "Execution is the highest
form of confidence."*

Your First Creation

Starting today, you'll run a five-day creation:

1. Pick your platform and niche.
2. Choose your message. What single problem do you solve?
3. Post or produce daily for five days. No expectations, just proof of action.
4. Document everything. Track progress, feedback, and insights.

This isn't about virality, it's about identity velocity. Every post, project, or conversation confirms: I am a creator now.

The Build Begins: You've stopped being a spectator.

Next, you'll uncover what you can monetise, your specialised knowledge, and the system to turn it into offers that pay.

THE EXTREME SKILL AUDIT

"The world doesn't pay for effort; it pays for clarity. The clearer your value, the faster the market finds you."

WHY SKILL AWARENESS EQUALS FREEDOM

Most people drown in potential because they never audit it. They've spent years building invisible equity—skills, experiences, insights but never stopped to recognise their market power.

The Extreme Skill Audit is how you make your value visible.

Skill Overview:

Type	Description	Market Impact	Example
Transferable Skill	Broad skills adaptable across industries	Medium	Communication, leadership, and time management
Specialised Skill	Specific expertise that solves a defined problem	High	Coaching, branding, performance systems
Experiential Skill	Knowledge earned through repetition of failure	Unique	Managing pressure, networking, and problem-solving

Step 1. Extract What You Already Know

Pull out a blank page. Make three columns:

1. Things I'm Good At = skills that come naturally or have been praised for.
2. Things I've Done Repeatedly = experiences or routines that built competence.
3. Problems I Can Solve for Others = outcomes people already ask you for help with.

Once it's all on paper, score each item on:
- Impact (Does this solve an urgent problem?)
- Enjoyment (Would I do this long-term?)
- Demand (Do people pay for this?)

Pro Insight: The overlap between "high impact" and "high demand" is your specialised knowledge zone, your unfair advantage.

Step 2. Map It: Skill → Solution → Offer

Skill-to-Solution Map:

Skill	Problem It Solves	Market Offer
Performance Coaching	Lack of discipline, low consistency	"90-Day Discipline Accelerator" program
Design Skills	Weak brand presence	Brand identity package
Networking Ability	Lack of clients or exposure	Business growth mastermind
Fitness Expertise	Inconsistent training results	Personal coaching or online course

Boss Law #13: Money flows to clarity, not talent.

Talent is potential energy. Clarity is kinetic energy; it moves markets. When you define your skills in terms of the problems they solve, you shift from being replaceable to being in demand.

Step 3. Validate With the Market

Your goal is not to perfect an idea, it's to test it fast. Find three people who could benefit from your skill. Ask them:

- What's your biggest struggle in this area?
- What would it be worth to fix it quickly?
- Have you ever paid for help before?

Those answers become your product outline. Not guesswork, data.

Mini Example: A video editor noticed small creators struggling with engagement. Instead of offering generic "editing," they positioned it as

"I help creators boost watch time by 40% through dynamic storytelling edits."

Result? 5 clients in 10 days: No ads, no website, just clarity and outreach.

Step 4. Rank and Refine

Go back to your audit list. Circle your top 3 skills that meet all three criteria:

- High Demand
- Solves Pain
- Energises You

Then define your Level of Leverage:

Level	Description	Focus
Direct skill	You do it yourself	Build proof & results
Teachable skill	You coach or teach others	Build brand authority
Systemised skill	You create assets, courses, or teams	Build scalability

Quote Callout: "Confusion kills cash flow, clarity creates it."

Step 5. The Skill Integration Plan

Now that you've identified your top 3 high-value skills:

1. Write your new "Value Sentence":
   "I help [who] achieve [result] using [skill]."
   Example: "I help busy professionals develop athlete-level focus through performance systems."

2. Integrate it into your identity.
   Use it in bios, intros, and pitches.

3. Document your transformation.

Share daily insights, lessons, and wins to demonstrate authority.

JOURNAL PROMPT

- What three skills have created the most results in your life?
- What problem do those skills solve for others?
- How can you package them clearly this week?
- What one offer can you test in the next 7 days?

You've uncovered your specialised knowledge. Next, you'll learn how to organise it into The Money Map. Your framework for translating value into consistent income and long-term freedom.

THE MONEY MAP & VISION FORMULA

Boss Law #14: "If you don't decide where your money goes, it will decide for you."

THE MONEY MAP: TURNING SKILLS INTO SYSTEMS

You've burned the old identity and discovered your specialised knowledge. Now it's time to organise your value into income flows, a structure that makes money predictable instead of accidental. Think of your Money Map as the GPS of your new life. It tells you:

- Where you are (your skills)
- Where you're going (your financial vision)
- How you'll get there (your offer systems)

Without a map, you work hard but drift.

With one, every action compounds toward financial freedom.

Step 1. Define Your Core Skill Stack

Write down your top three high-value skills from your audit. Then connect each skill to a clear result it creates for others.

Example:

Skill	Result Created	Potential Offer	Price Range
Performance Systems	Consistency & discipline	"90-day execution blueprint" program	$500 - $2000
Branding & Design	Strong visual identity	Brand starter package	$250 - $1500
Fitness Coaching	Better energy & focus	Corporate wellness consulting	$1000 - $3000

Now you can see your value translated into offers. That's your first step towards scalable income.

Step 2. Create the 3-Tier Income Structure

Every Boss needs three levels of value creation:

1. Base Income (Foundation) – Your quick-cash skill or service (e.g., freelancing, 1-on-1 coaching).
2. Build Income (Growth) – A repeatable package or program that delivers a consistent result.
3. Breakthrough Income (Leverage) – Products, systems, or teams that let you earn while scaling.

The Money Pyramid:

Breakthrough Income (Leverage)

↑

Build Income (Systems)

↑

Base Income (Cash Flow)

The goal isn't to skip steps. You master one layer, then stack. Each level multiplies. Do not replace the previous one.

Step 3. Assign Dollar Goals with Purpose

Money without direction burns fast. Give every dollar an assignment:

- Survival – Bills, food, living costs.
- Freedom – Savings, debt clearing, and emergency fund.
- Growth – Education, marketing, brand assets.
- Impact – Family, giving, legacy projects.

When your money has purpose, discipline becomes automatic. You no longer chase motivation; you follow a mission.

Step 4. The Vision Formula

This is where you shift from income goals to identity design. There are three layers of vision every Boss builds:

1. Identity Vision — Who You're Becoming
Ask yourself: "What does the 'Boss Version' of me look like, think like, and act like?"

Define:
- Your daily non-negotiables
- The standards you operate from
- What you no longer tolerate

> Boss Law #15: "Your standards are
> the ceiling of your results."

2. Impact Vision — Who You Serve
True bosses build influence by solving pain.

Your vision should answer:
- Who am I helping?
- What problem am I solving for them?
- How does their life improve because I exist?

When your purpose and service connect, you build brand gravity, and people start coming to you instead of you chasing them.

3. Freedom Vision — How You Live
What does financial and lifestyle freedom mean to you personally?

- Work from anywhere?
- Time with family or creative projects?
- No longer trading hours for income?

Freedom isn't a fantasy; it's a target. Once written, every decision becomes easier:
"Does this get me closer to that vision?"

Step 5. The Money Map in Action

Let's connect it all with a short real-world case example:

A fitness coach with a background in sports realised his specialised knowledge was discipline under pressure. He packaged this into a "Focus & Execution System" for entrepreneurs, priced at $499. After 10 beta clients and excellent results, he built a digital version ($99) and hired an assistant to automate onboarding. In 90 days, he moved from 1-on-1 sessions to semi-passive income, all because his Money Map was clear.

ACTION BLUEPRINT: YOUR MONEY MAP SETUP

- Identify your three core skills.
- Map each to a specific problem and offer.
- Set income tiers (Base, Build, Breakthrough).

- Assign purpose to your money flow.
- Write your Identity, Impact, and Freedom Visions.

"Without clarity, there is no cash flow. Without vision, there is no momentum."

JOURNAL PROMPT

- What does your ideal Boss life look like 30 days from now? 6 months? 2 years?
- What three skills can fund that life right now?
- What must you stop doing to make space for your Boss Vision?

Your Money Map is your new operating system. You now understand what you offer, why it matters, and how to turn it into consistent income.

Next, you'll step into Day 2 – Weaponise Your Value. Where you build your first irresistible offer and turn clarity into cash.

DAY 2
WEAPONISE YOUR VALUE

Boss Law #16: "Clarity turns confidence
into currency. Skill becomes power
only when it's packaged and sold."

TUESDAY MORNING: FROM DISCIPLINE TO DIRECTION

The second sunrise hits differently. Yesterday, you tore down the old self. The version that waited for permission, blamed circumstance, or mistook activity for progress.

Today you're building with precision. You can feel it, the calm before the pivot. The shift from discipline to direction.

As an athlete, I lived by structure—training schedules, feedback loops, relentless repetition. When I stepped into entrepreneurship, I realised business is no different: You still show up, measure, adjust, and perform. The only difference is that now your mind is the field.

Boss Law #17: Effort is cheap. Precision is rare.
The difference is control.

The reason most talented people stay stuck is because their value is undefined. They're running drills with no scoreboard. They're producing effort, not outcomes.

Today, you weaponise what you already know. You'll package your skills into something people will pay for, not out of charity, but because it solves a real problem. This isn't about selling. It's about translating ability into transformation.

THE DIFFERENCE BETWEEN TALENT AND LEVERAGE

Talent is potential energy. Leverage is motion. You're not paid for how hard you work, you're paid for how clearly you solve.

When I first built my academy, I thought parents were paying for drills and training sessions. They weren't. They were buying confidence, a structured path for their kids to improve. The skill was football. The value was transformation and trust. That realisation changed everything. In business, people aren't paying for your task; they're paying for the result of your clarity.

> Boss Law #18: Value unspoken is invisible,
> value unstructured is worthless.

FROM SKILLED TO PAID

The market doesn't reward talent; it rewards clarity. And clarity means knowing exactly three things:

1. Who do you serve?
2. What problem do you solve?
3. What outcome do you guarantee?

The gap between "skilled" and "paid" is simply a definition.

Many professionals think they have a sales problem when, in fact, they have a communication problem. If the world can't repeat your offer in one sentence, you don't have one yet. Take ten minutes and write the answer to this:

"If someone asked what you do, could you explain the result you create, not the work you perform, in one breath?"

Until you can, you're still playing defense.

Real-World Case Study: The Designer Who Simplified

A young designer kept chasing trends. Logos, social posts, and flyers for tiny pay. Then she realised clients didn't want "design." They wanted trust in their image. She built a 7-Day Brand Starter Kit: a logo, a color palette, and three templates. The deliverable stayed the same; the value frame changed. Within 30 days, she tripled her income. Why? Because she packaged clarity, not chaos. That's what Day 2 is about: Transforming chaos into clarity, and clarity into cash.

THE BOSS OFFER FORMULA

Every sale in history runs on one thing: a promise. When your promise is precise, believable, and valuable, it becomes magnetic.

Your offer is the bridge between what you know and what others need. Here's the framework I still use in every program and partnership.

1. The Promise (Outcome)

Make one promise.
Solve one problem.
Serve one audience.

Use the Boss Sentence Formula: "I help [WHO] achieve [RESULT] in [TIMEFRAME] without [COMMON PAIN]."

Example:
- "I help footballers develop elite skills in 30 days without relying on overcrowded team sessions."

Specificity sells.

Boss Law #19: If you can't describe the outcome in one breath, you don't own it.

2. The Mechanism (How You Deliver)

This is your system. Name it. Own it. Teach it. When I built my first training system, I called it The Elite Player Pathway. Same exercises, same drills, but structured, named, and repeatable. That name turned process into property.

Other examples:
- The Elite Edge System
- The Fast-Track Football Formula
- The Pro-Level Acceleration Model
- The Focus Reset Protocol

People don't pay for coaching; they pay for systems that promise certainty.

3. The Proof (Why Believe You)

If they don't trust you, they won't transact. Proof can come from:
- Results you've delivered (even small wins).
- Background credibility (your track record).
- Process evidence ("here's the checklist we follow").

Boss Law #20: Transparency converts faster than theatrics.

4. The Terms (Price, Timeline, Risk Reversal)

Your offer should feel structured, not slippery.

Spell out:
- Duration
- Deliverables
- Price
- Risk reversal (if any)

Example: "This is a 30-day program. Four strategy sessions, a daily tracker, and feedback access. If you complete every checkpoint and don't see measurable progress, I'll extend another week at no cost."

That's authority, not arrogance.
It tells the client: I believe in this process enough to share the risk.

Example Offer: The 30-Day Elite Player Pathway
- Promise: Become a sharper, faster, more dangerous footballer in 30 days—with results showing within two weeks.
- Mechanism: Two weekly high-performance sessions + personalised training plan + skill-tracking system.
- Proof: 100+ footballers upgraded their technique and match impact.
- Terms: $500; if you follow the system and don't improve, we'll add an extra week with no charge.

Boss Law #21: Confidence isn't declared;
it's demonstrated through structure.

THE VALUE LADDER: FROM ENTRY TO EMPIRE

Once your first offer is clear, the next step is scale. You build depth before width. A ladder of value lets buyers choose their own commitment level; you just meet them where they are.

I learned this lesson while building my coaching programs. Parents wanted low-commitment trials first, then advanced sessions once trust formed.

That same psychology works everywhere.

Tier 1: Entry ($50 – $100)
Quick win offers.
They prove value and collect data.
Examples: 30-minute consultation, 7-Day Starter Plan, mini audit.

Tier 2: Core ($500 – $1000)

Your main transformation.

High-touch yet repeatable.

Examples: 30-Day Performance Reset, Brand Identity Sprint, Content-to-Client System.

Tier 3: Flagship ($2500 – $10,000)

Premium results for premium clients.

This is mentorship, a done-for-you service, or a team install.

Examples: 90-Day Authority Accelerator, Founder's Operating System, Elite Performance Program.

> **Boss Law #22: You don't need 100 products;
> you need one pathway that pays you
> 100 ways.**

Every client becomes a future testimonial, and every testimonial becomes your next sale.

> **Boss Law #23: "You can't deposit potential.
> You can only deposit execution."**

FROM IDEA → INCOME IN 48 HOURS

Yesterday, you built clarity. Today you'll build proof. Bosses don't wait for permission; they test reality. This is where your offer leaves the notebook and hits the market.

You're going to validate fast. Prove that people want what you sell before you waste months building the perfect version.

When I first started coaching athletes, I didn't have a big program. I had one framework and one promise. I tested it with three people—not a website, not ads, just direct messages and phone calls.

Within 48 hours, I had my first paid clients. That proof was worth more than any logo or business plan.

Boss Law #24: Money loves speed and clarity.

PRICING CONFIDENCE CHECKLIST

Most people undercharge because they confuse self-worth with market value.

Pricing isn't about what you think you're worth; it's about the outcome you deliver and the belief you stand behind it.

The 5-Step Pricing Reset

1. Anchor to the Outcome
   Ask: "How much is this result worth to my client?"
   Example: If your system saves a business owner 5 hours a week, that's 20 hours a month. What's 20 hours of their time worth?

2. Set Your Minimum Standard
   Decide on the lowest amount that motivates you to overdeliver. Anything below that erodes your energy.

3. Benchmark Competitors
   Not to copy, but to position. If you're cheaper than everyone, you're telling the market you don't believe in your own result.

4. Price on Transformation, Not Time
   People pay for outcomes, not hours. Stop charging $30/hour and start charging $300 for a result.

5. State Price Calmly, Then Pause
   Silence sells. The most powerful close is confidence without nervous justification.

Boss Law #25: Your price is a mirror of
your certainty.

PRODUCTISING YOUR SKILL: FROM SERVICE TO SYSTEM

The key to freedom is productisation, turning what you do once into something that can run without you. Every Boss builds systems, not jobs.

The Three Levels of Productisation

Level	Description	Example
1. Service	Manual execution of your skill	You design logos for clients
2. Systemised Service	Standardised process with templates and deliverables	You offer a 7-day brand starter kit
3. Productised Offer	Fixed scope, fixed price, repeatable delivery	The "logo & launch" package: 3 logos, brand guide, social kit

Boss Law #26: If you can't repeat it,
you can't scale it.

Start documenting everything you do for clients. Turn it into templates, checklists, and frameworks. That's your first intellectual asset, your tangible wealth.

MVP FAST TEST: VALIDATE YOUR OFFER IN 48 HOURS

Forget months of building. You're going to get honest feedback and real cash flow now.

Step-by-Step Validation Blueprint

Step 1: Outline Your Offer

Write your Boss Sentence: "I help [WHO] achieve [RESULT] in [TIMEFRAME] without [PAIN]."

Step 2: Find 10 Potential Clients
List people you already know who fit this description—friends, colleagues, followers, old network. You don't need an audience. You need relevance.

Step 3: Reach Out Directly (Cold DM Template)
"Hey [name], I'm testing a new [program/service] that helps [ideal result]. I'm offering it to 3 people this week at a discount in exchange for feedback. Would you like the details?"

Simple. Direct. Zero fluff.

Step 4: Deliver One Quick Win
Show proof fast—a PDF, a video breakdown, a plan, a result within 24 hours.

Step 5: Collect Feedback & Testimonials
Screenshots, quotes, DMs—all fuel for your next launch.

Nothing sells like "real people, real results."

**Boss Law #27: Data beats doubt.
Always test with reality.**

UNDERSTANDING VALUE VS PRICE

Price is what they pay. Value is what they get. Never confuse the two. You can sell a $50 offer that feels worth $500 or a $500 offer that feels like $50. The difference is delivery and perception.

Ask yourself:
- Does my offer reduce pain or increase pleasure instantly?
- Does it save time, money, energy, or status?
- Do I make them feel seen, understood, and safe to decide?

When you focus on felt value, price becomes secondary.

**Boss Law #28: If you can quantify their pain,
you can justify your price.**

THE PSYCHOLOGY OF AN IRRESISTIBLE OFFER

Every offer lives or dies by emotion. People buy emotionally and justify logically. To create irresistible offers, stack these five psychological triggers:

1. Speed — "Get results in 7 days or less."
2. Certainty — "Here's exactly what you'll get and when."
3. Simplicity — "Three steps, no guesswork."
4. Scarcity — "Only three spots this week."
5. Safety — "Redo guarantee if you don't see results."

Combine those, and your offer sells before you speak.

**Boss Law #29: Emotion starts the sale.
Logic confirms it.**

PLUG-AND-PLAY MINI SWIPE FILE

Use these as templates for posts or messages today.

Example #1: Social Post

"I'm helping 3 [ideal clients] get [results] in [timeframe] using my [system name].

If you've been trying to [solve problem], DM me 'READY' and I'll send details."

Example #2: Email

Subject: [First Name], let's make [Result] happen this week.

I'm launching a new [program/product] that helps [WHO] achieve [RESULT] without [PAIN].

Three spots only this week for founding members—you'll get direct access and a discount in exchange for feedback.

Want details? Hit reply with 'YES'.

Example #3: Offer Post

"Your idea isn't stuck. It's just unpackaged. Here's how I turn [skills] into income with The Boss Offer Formula. Comment 'BOSS' and I'll send you the exact framework."

ACTION BLUEPRINT: POLISH YOUR FIRST OFFER

- Step 1: Refine your Boss Sentence.
- Step 2: Set a minimum price that feels powerful.
- Step 3: Build your simple delivery system (template or checklist).
- Step 4: Reach out to 10 potential clients today.
- Step 5: Validate within 48 hours—collect feedback and proof.

JOURNAL PROMPT: REWRITE YOUR VALUE INTO A WEAPON

- What transformation am I truly selling?
- How can I make that result inevitable for my client?
- What system name or identity represents my process?
- How can I raise my price without adding complexity?
- What would I charge if I believed 100% in my value today?

Write honestly and don't overthink. This isn't about ego, it's about ownership.

END-OF-DAY REFLECTION

Today, you learned to define, test, and validate your value in the real world. You turned discipline into direction and direction into revenue.

Boss Law #30: Money flows to clarity, speed, and structure.

Tomorrow, you enter Day 3 — Maximum Visibility, Minimum Time, where you learn to turn your offer into a magnet for attention, authority, and sales.

Day 3
MAXIMUM VISIBILITY, MINIMUM TIME

Boss Law #31: "Obscurity is the silent killer of potential. The world can't buy from you if it doesn't know you exist."

THE LAW OF OBSCURITY

Imagine this: You've got the skill, the discipline, the knowledge, but your phone's quiet. You've built something of value, but no one's talking about it. You're the best-kept secret in your field, and secrets don't get paid. Most people don't fail because they lack talent or work ethic. They fail because no one knows they exist. This is the day we fix that.

Visibility is the bridge between your value and your income. You can have the best product, the most life-changing service, the cleanest system, but if no one sees it, it's invisible. Obscurity, not competition, is your real enemy.

THE VISIBILITY MINDSET

When I left sport and stepped into business, I learned something fast. Performance doesn't guarantee recognition.

In football, you could play flawlessly, but if you weren't visible to the scouts or agents, your career stalled. Entrepreneurship is the same. The market rewards attention, not quite perfection.

The fix? Treat visibility as your daily discipline. Visibility isn't vanity. It's a service. It's how you help people discover the solution they didn't know they needed—you.

**Boss Law #32: If you stay invisible,
you stay replaceable.**

Phase 1: The Visibility Equation

Visibility = Message × Consistency × Platforms × Proof

1. Message — What you stand for. Your transformation story and core offer.
2. Consistency — Showing up even when you don't feel like it.
3. Platforms — Where your audience already pays attention.
4. Proof — Real results, testimonials, transformations.

Master those four elements, and your name becomes synonymous with your value.

Phase 2: The 80/20 Visibility Strategy

You don't need to be everywhere; you need to be where it matters. The top 20% of platforms drive 80% of your exposure and income.

The Buyer's Habitat Map:

Platform	Buyer Intent	Ideal Content Type	Example
Instagram / TikTok / Facebook	Fast emotional connection	Quick transformations, before/after clips	Fitness, coaching, design
LinkedIn	Business credibility	Case studies, value threads	Consulting, B2B, marketing
YouTube / Podcast	Long-form trust	Teaching frameworks	Mentorship, education
Emails / DMs	Conversion	Offers, personal invites	All niches

Find your buyer's habitat, go where they already hang out. That's your hunting ground.

Boss Law #33: Stop shouting into empty rooms. Speak where buyers listen.

Phase 3: The Authority System

Goal: Build instant trust through repetition, proof, and clarity.

Step 1: Anchor Your Core Message
Your message should answer three questions fast:
- Who do you help?
- What problem do you solve?
- What outcome do you create?

Example: "I help ambitious professionals turn specialised skills into income within 5 days."

It's clean, repeatable, and instantly tells people why they should listen.

Step 2: Post for Proof, Not Praise
You're not chasing likes, you're building authority through evidence.

Types of proof-based posts:
- Process posts: "Here's how I built this."
- Result posts: "Here's what my client achieved."
- Teaching posts: "Here's what you can learn from this."
- Personal reflections: "Here's the mindset that changed everything."

Each one builds micro-trust. People buy because they feel you can guide them, not because your graphics look perfect.

Step 3: The 7-Day Authority Blueprint
A visibility blueprint is about consistency, not perfection. You're building momentum through simple repetition.

Day	Action	Focus
Monday	Post your message	Establish positioning
Tuesday	Share your process	Show behind the scenes
Wednesday	Drop quick win content	Give immediate value
Thursday	Share proof/testimonial	Build credibility
Friday	Direct offer post	Invite conversations
Saturday	Engage with others' posts	Build relationships
Sunday	Reflect + Plan	Review analytics, reset system

Run this for 4 weeks, and you'll notice something shift. You'll stop chasing attention and start attracting opportunity.

Boss Law #34: Repetition builds reputation.

Phase 4: Authority Through Consistency

In sport, consistency wins championships. In business, it builds empires. Visibility isn't about going viral once; it's about being remembered daily.

Show up like a professional:
- Schedule content like training sessions.
- Track metrics like game stats.
- Treat feedback like match film—study, adjust, improve.

Discipline turns visibility into predictability. A professional doesn't ask, "Do I feel like showing up?" They ask, "What's today's play?"

Phase 5: Your Visibility Identity

Before others believe in your authority, you must embody it. Every post, message, and conversation is a chance to reinforce who you are.

Ask yourself:
- Does my content look like it's coming from a leader or a follower?
- Do my words create certainty or confusion?
- Do I project energy, clarity, and conviction?

You don't need to fake confidence. You build it through consistent proof of action.

Boss Law #35: Your energy sells before your words do.

Case Study: Building Trust From the Ground Up

When I transitioned from playing to business, I wasn't loud online. I was focused on results. But I learned quickly: discipline and silence don't attract clients.

When I started sharing my process, short clips from coaching sessions, player results, or lessons on mindset, I began to see momentum. It wasn't overnight. It was rhythm.

Every post wasn't a sales pitch—it was a signal: I'm here. I'm consistent. I deliver. Within weeks, parents started messaging. Players referred friends. Local coaches reached out for collaborations. That's how visibility compounds, not from flash, but from frequency.

Phase 6: The Boss Visibility Stack

There are three layers of visibility every modern entrepreneur must build:

1. Anchor Content (Authority)
   Longer, educational content that demonstrates leadership.
   Examples: videos, carousels, podcasts.

2. Proof Content (Credibility)
   Screenshots, testimonials, transformation stories.

3. Engagement Content (Connection)
   Behind-the-scenes, short stories, lessons learned.

Each layer works together to create trust at scale.

**Boss Law #36: People buy from momentum,
not mystery.**

Phase 7: The Energy Equation

Visibility without energy is invisible. Every word, clip, and post transmits your state. Speak with conviction, not desperation. Write like someone who knows they can change lives because you can.

If you sound unsure, they'll feel unsure. Confidence is contagious.

Remember: you don't have to convince people. You have to communicate belief.

**Boss Law #37: Certainty converts.
Energy amplifies.**

Today, you discovered that visibility isn't luck; it's a system. It's the daily discipline of showing up, sharing, and serving until your name equals value. You don't need followers. You need believers, and belief starts with consistency.

We'll now take this foundation and turn it into systems and proof engines that scale your visibility even when you're offline.

You'll learn how to transform one result into ten new clients, build partnerships through mutual trust, and design a Visibility Blueprint that runs like clockwork.

AUTHORITY IN ACTION & NETWORK EXPANSION

> Boss Law #38: "You don't get paid for what you know, you get paid for what people believe you can deliver."

THE NEW CURRENCY: CREDIBILITY

At this stage, you're visible. People are starting to notice what you're doing. But visibility without credibility is noise.

Anyone can post. Few can prove consistency.

This part is where you make people believe in your brand, not through hype, but through evidence, structure, and experience.

Your goal today is not to "look like a boss." Your goal is to become a trusted authority, the person who delivers every time. And trust, once built, makes selling easy and scaling inevitable.

> Boss Law #39: The most powerful brand in any market is the one that delivers what it promises, every single time.

BUILDING BELIEF THROUGH EXPERIENCE

Authority isn't something you claim. It's something you earn. It's built through outcomes, consistency, and transformation. Forget fake reviews or paid shoutouts. Authority comes from your track record, even if it starts small.

If you helped one person achieve something, that's the start of your authority engine. You take that win, refine the system, and scale it.

THE AUTHORITY LOOP

1. Do the Work — Get your first result (for yourself or someone else).
2. Document the Process — Show how it happened step-by-step.
3. Deliver Consistently — Repeat the process and make it predictable.
4. Distill It — Turn your method into a framework, guide, or product.

This loop transforms you from "just another business owner" to a trusted leader in your field.

Boss Law #40: Results are your resume.

FROM PRODUCT TO PLATFORM: TURNING WHAT YOU SELL INTO A BRAND

Whether you're selling a service (like coaching, design, consulting) or a product (like fitness gear, templates, digital courses, or apparel), your goal is the same: Make people associate your name with transformation.

A business transaction earns money.

A brand relationship earns trust and long-term income.

Example: The Dual Approach

Let's say you run a sports academy. You're providing a service—training athletes.

But you could also build product extensions:

- A branded online course on "Discipline & Performance Training."
- A physical product line: Branded gear or recovery tools.
- A digital training planner app.

Now, your name doesn't just represent a service. It represents an ecosystem.

Each product feeds the next. Each customer becomes part of a growing movement.

Boss Law #41: A brand isn't what you sell, it's what people say about you when you're not in the room.

THE CREDIBILITY TRIANGLE: STORY, SYSTEM, AND SOCIAL PROOF

To dominate your market, you must show three kinds of credibility:

1. Story Credibility

   Your journey matters. Not for ego, for relatability. When people understand why you do what you do, they connect emotionally. But always keep it tight, no "rags-to-riches" cliches.

   You're not here to impress. You're here to inspire action. Your background and discipline already do that—structure, mindset, teamwork, repetition. Those principles are timeless in business.

2. System Credibility

   People trust systems. Document your method, how you deliver results and make it replicable. If you help clients, outline your "3-Step Performance Method."

If you sell a product, show your testing process, reviews, and standards. If you coach, show your transformation roadmap. Your system is your silent salesman.

3. Social Credibility

Leverage testimonials, collaborations, media features, or public client results. Each acts as external validation; it signals trust faster than ads ever could.

> **Boss Law #42: A story opens the door.
> A system builds the house.**

NETWORK ECONOMICS: BUILDING CIRCLES THAT BUILD YOU

You can't build an empire alone. You need connections that compound momentum. But networking isn't about handshakes and business cards, it's about strategic proximity.

The key is to surround yourself with people who are already playing the game at the next level, and then find a way to add value before you ever ask for anything.

The "Proximity Leverage" Framework

1. Identify: Who are five people already trusted in your space
2. Engage: Support, share, or comment with genuine insights.
3. Contribute: Offer something useful—a skill, collaboration, or introduction.
4. Elevate: Once the relationship is built, explore partnerships or joint projects.

> **Boss Law #43: Your income mirrors
> your inner circle.**

When you consistently offer value and operate at a high standard, you attract high-standard people. It's magnetism, not chasing.

COLLABORATION SYSTEMS: TURNING RELATIONSHIPS INTO REVENUE

Collaboration multiplies reach, credibility, and audience trust.

Here's how to use it strategically, not desperately.

Types of Collaboration

- Joint Promotions: Team up with someone complementary—fitness + nutrition, coach + mindset mentor, product + service.
- Affiliate Models: Offer a commission to trusted partners who refer sales.
- Guest Training or Interviews: Share your message on their audience's platform.
- Micro-Events: Run joint webinars or pop-up challenges.

Each collab must serve three goals:
1. Mutual Value — both audiences win.
2. Aligned Brand — same values, same energy.
3. Clear Offer — something to act on immediately.

Example

You collaborate with a local supplement brand for your academy athletes. They supply free samples for a trial group. You share results and tag them; they feature your program in their marketing. Both audiences grow. No ads. No cost. Pure synergy.

Boss Law #44: Collaboration done right is multiplication, not dilution.

VISIBILITY SYSTEMS 2.0: AUTOMATING ATTENTION

You've built momentum, but to scale, you must systemise attention. Otherwise, you'll burn out trying to stay "online."

The 3-Part Visibility Rhythm

1. Batch: Create your week's content in one sitting (2–3 hours).
2. Automate: Schedule posts using tools like Notion, Later, or Metricool.
3. Engage: Spend 30 minutes daily replying and connecting authentically.

Set your brand rhythm like a training program. Consistent, measurable, effective.

Example:

- Monday: Publish educational or authority content.
- Wednesday: Post behind-the-scenes or product results.
- Friday: Invite engagement or highlight client transformations.

By Week 4, you'll have automated visibility while focusing on delivery.

**Boss Law #45: The disciplined brand
beats the loud brand.**

THE 7-DAY MOMENTUM CHALLENGE

This is your end-of-day execution plan. Each day, you'll plant seeds that grow into attention, sales, and brand strength.

Day	Mission	Action
Monday	Authority post	Teach your framework or product's core benefit
Tuesday	Credibility	Share one win, result, or transformation
Wednesday	Network	Engage with 10 leaders or peers in your space
Thursday	Collaboration	DM 3 people with partnership ideas
Friday	Product push	Launch one piece of content linking to your offer
Saturday	Reflection	Audit your visibility data
Sunday	Recharge	Plan next week's batch of content

Run this challenge. You'll not only grow your visibility but also start attracting referrals, collabs, and repeat sales automatically.

Boss Law #46: Momentum compounds when you act before you're ready.

JOURNAL PROMPTS

- What can I show today that builds trust without speaking a word?
- Which product or service do people associate me with right now, and is that aligned with where I'm going?
- Who could I collaborate with to elevate both our brands?
- What's one system I could automate this week to save time and stay consistent?

END OF DAY REFLECTION

By now, you've turned visibility into trust and momentum into structure. You've learned that credibility doesn't come from followers; it comes from execution, reputation, and relationships.

Tomorrow, we enter Day 4 – Sell Like a Boss, where you'll learn how to turn that credibility into conversions. Mastering tonality, energy, and influence without ever sounding "salesy."

Boss Law #47: You're not chasing clients anymore, you're attracting believers.

DAY 4
SELL LIKE A BOSS

"People don't buy products. They buy certainty."

THE MOMENT EVERYTHING CHANGES

It's Thursday morning.

You've spent the week tearing down limits, rewriting your identity, and discovering your actual value. You've started speaking louder, standing taller, and acting like your goals already belong to you.

But now comes the test.

Because this is the day the world responds. All week you've been building: ideas, offers, systems. Now, you must influence. And make no mistake, selling is not about manipulating anyone into saying yes. It's about leading people to make decisions in their own best interests.

The true Boss doesn't chase; they create clarity. They don't push, they pull. They don't sell, they align.

This is where every ambitious entrepreneur, coach, and creator separates themselves from the noise. You're not trying to convince. You're trying to communicate truth. Clearly, powerfully, and with certainty.

Boss Law #48: When your energy leads with clarity, selling becomes effortless.

FROM SELLING TO LEADING

Every amateur focuses on "closing." Every professional focuses on "guiding." The difference? Pressure vs. Presence.

Selling feels heavy when you make it about you. When you're worried about "getting the sale," your energy collapses inward. You start grasping for control instead of projecting it.

The shift happens the moment you understand this: You are not asking people to give you money. You are giving them an opportunity to move closer to the life they want. That's what leadership is.

Sales is leadership, condensed into a conversation.

Boss Law #49: True sales mastery is calm leadership disguised as conversation.

WHY MOST PEOPLE HATE SELLING

Because they've experienced it done wrong. They've felt the awkward tension of someone trying too hard—the forced script, the nervous tone, the lack of confidence.

The irony?

Those same people are now terrified to sell themselves, even when their product or service could change lives.

That's where you come in. Because today, you'll learn to do it right. We're going to weaponise integrity, turning your authenticity into authority.

You'll sell through clarity, not chaos. Through certainty, not scripts. Through value, not volume.

THE BOSS INFLUENCE FRAMEWORK

<u>Connect</u> → <u>Clarify</u> → <u>Create Desire</u> → <u>Confirm</u> → <u>Close</u>

This is your new foundation. Simple, elegant, and deadly effective. Each step builds on the psychology of trust and human decision-making. Let's break it down.

CONNECT: Build Instant Emotional Trust

Before any transaction, there's emotion. Before emotion, there's energy. You're not selling words, you're selling presence.

From the first message, call, or conversation, people subconsciously ask:
- "Do I trust this person?"
- "Do they understand me?"
- "Can they actually help me?"

Your goal is to answer yes without saying a word.

Boss Connection Moves:
- Mirror energy, not personality.
- Lead with curiosity: ask, don't assume.
- Be human, stories beat scripts every time.

Example:

When someone says, "I've been struggling to grow my business," don't reply with your offer. Say, "Tell me more about what's been holding you back."

That single sentence establishes leadership. You're guiding the frame.

CLARIFY: Define the Real Problem

People rarely know their actual problem. They'll come to you saying, "I need more followers," when what they really need is a clear offer. Or "I need to lose weight," when what they really want is self-respect. Clarifying is where the professional separates from the amateur.

Amateurs sell solutions.

Bosses sell understanding.

Boss Clarification Moves:
- Use the "Why 3 Times" rule. Ask why until the emotional core reveals itself.
- Restate what they said better than they said it. That builds instant authority.
- Never solve too early; tension creates value.

CREATE DESIRE: Paint the Vision

Now comes emotion. This is where you show them what's possible, the transformation. You don't push benefits. You paint futures.

In neuroscience terms, the brain buys emotion, then justifies it with logic.

Example phrases that build emotional momentum:
- "Imagine waking up knowing this is already handled."
- "How would it feel to finally be free from that stress?"
- "What would it mean for your family if this worked?"

Notice, each line moves the focus from price to possibility.

That's persuasion done right.

CONFIRM: The Alignment Phase

Before you close, you check alignment. This is where amateurs rush: Bosses breathe.

Ask:

- "Does this sound like what you've been looking for?"
- "Do you feel this direction makes sense for you?"

This gives your prospect ownership of the decision.

You're not selling anymore, you're confirming partnership. It also reduces objections because you've eliminated internal conflict before it arises.

CLOSE: The Calm Command

This isn't where pressure happens; it's where peace happens. When you've done the first four stages right, the close becomes natural.

Boss Closers don't sound like:
"So, are you ready to buy?"

They sound like:
"Let's get started—I'll send over the setup link right now."

It's calm. It's confident. It's assumed. You're not asking for permission, you're leading them through a decision they've already made emotionally.

> **Boss Law #50: Confidence isn't about being loud, it's about being certain.**

THE PSYCHOLOGY OF DECISION

People buy based on emotion, justify with logic, and stay loyal because of identity. Your job is to lead them through those three levels: emotion → logic → identity.

Let's break it down:

1. Emotion: The Spark
   You trigger emotion by reflecting their problem vividly. The more they feel understood, the more their brain releases oxytocin, the trust hormone.

2. Logic: The Safety Net
   Now their rational mind needs reassurance: proof, clarity, simplicity. You show process, not promises. You say, "Here's how it works step by step." The structure is safe.

3. Identity: The Lock-In
   The final layer is self-image. When someone buys, they're voting for a new version of themselves. You help them see that the act of buying is actually becoming. That's elite sales psychology, guiding people to a decision that aligns with who they want to be.

**Boss Law #51: Emotion opens the door,
logic walks them through, identity locks it in.**

Case Study: From Passion to Profit

Meet Alex—a coach running a local football academy. He doesn't sell training, he sells transformation. Parents come to him thinking they're buying sessions. But what they're really buying is confidence, discipline, and community for their kids. By communicating that deeper outcome, he turns hesitant leads into loyal clients, not through pressure, but through purpose.

He leads conversations the same way he leads players: With calm, certainty, and belief. That's selling like a Boss.

Boss Law #52: The highest form of selling
is serving with conviction.

OBJECTION ALCHEMY, TONALITY & DAILY INFLUENCE SYSTEMS

Boss Law #53: Persuasion begins long before
the pitch; it starts the moment you decide to
show up as the person worth listening to.

SCENE: THURSDAY EVENING, THE TURNING POINT

It's Thursday afternoon. The glow of your screen reflects a DM thread, half-finished. Your fingers hover over the keyboard. The person on the other side isn't just a prospect, they're proof that your visibility works.

This moment defines the difference between those who "talk about" selling and those who become trusted closers. You take a breath and remind yourself: Confidence doesn't come from knowing every script; it comes from knowing your worth.

THE SAVAGE MINDSET OF OBJECTION ALCHEMY

Objections aren't rejection, they're curiosity wearing armor. When someone says "I need to think about it", "It's not the right time", or "I can't afford it", what they're really saying is:

"I don't yet trust that this will work for me."

A Boss never argues; they uncover. They don't push; they pull clarity to the surface.

THE 5-STEP OBJECTION ALCHEMY SYSTEM

1. Pause and Acknowledge
   Never rush an objection. Silence creates gravity. "That's totally fair—
   I hear that a lot. Can I ask what's holding you back most?"

2. Clarify the Core Concern
   Most objections hide a deeper layer—fear of loss, fear of failure, or
   lack of clarity. "So it's not really about the price—it's about making
   sure it actually gets you the result you want, right?"

3. Reframe with Logic + Emotion
   Logic convinces the mind; emotion moves the body. "That's exactly
   why people invest—they're tired of wasting time doing it the slow
   way."

4. Anchor with Proof of Possibility
   Use micro-examples, short and real. "One of my students said the
   same thing last week. He leaped, and within 48 hours, booked his
   first client."

5. Close with Calm Certainty
   "If you're ready, let's make this simple. I'll send the link now—we'll
   get started today."

> Boss Law #54: You don't overcome
> objections; you dissolve them by making
> belief stronger than fear.

TONALITY: THE INVISIBLE SALES WEAPON

You can say the right words with the wrong tone and lose the deal.
Tonality is the emotional fingerprint of persuasion. It communicates
certainty, warmth, and authority before logic ever enters the room.

Tone Type	When To Use	Example
Certainty	When giving directions	"Here's what's going to happen next."
Curiosity	When asking qualifying questions	"Tell me more about what's been holding you back."
Empathy	When handling objections	"I completely understand, this has to feel right for you."
Inspiration	When closing	"This is the moment where everything starts to shift."

Boss Law #55: Tonality sells trust before words sell value.

Micro-Exercise: The Mirror Drill

1. Record yourself saying your Boss Offer sentence.
2. Listen to it back. Does it sound like you believe it?
3. Repeat until it carries confidence, calmness, and conviction.

Communication Mastery: The DM-to-Call Bridge

Step 1: Warm Connection
Start with a genuine comment or value-based question. "Hey [Name], saw your post about [topic], loved how you broke that down."

Step 2: Bridge the Gap
Lead into relevance. "Out of curiosity, what's your main goal with [problem] right now?"

Step 3: Shift to Solution Mode
Once they engage, move to a clear call to action. "I've helped others solve this exact issue—want me to share how we did it?"

Step 4: Invite to Call or Offer
"If it sounds good, let's hop on a quick call—I'll see if it's a fit."

Boss Law #56: Sales conversations aren't transactions; they're transformations for both sides.

The Power of Presence

Whether it's a DM, Zoom call, or face-to-face, your presence is felt before your words are heard.

Presence = Energy × Focus.

- Eliminate background distractions.
- Slow your breathing before speaking.
- Match the prospect's energy, then lead it slightly higher.

Boss Law #57: Presence turns attention into trust. Trust turns curiosity into action.

Case Study: The Moment of Belief

A fitness coach hesitated on calls; she knew her system worked, but hated "selling." She practiced objection alchemy for one week. Her next call? She stayed calm, reframed an objection, and closed a $2,000 program in 12 minutes. The secret wasn't new tactics—it was tonality + certainty.

DAILY INFLUENCE SYSTEMS

Influence isn't built in bursts; it's forged in rhythm. Here's your daily influence rhythm (20-minute system):

1. 5 min — Mindset Tune-In:
   Read your Boss Affirmations aloud. ("People need what I offer. I'm not chasing—I'm choosing.")

2. 5 min — DM Outreach:
   Connect with three warm leads using the DM Bridge.

3. 5 min — Voice Practice:
   Record and listen to your Boss Offer sentence. Sharpen your tone, pacing, and clarity.

4. 5 min — Sales Review:
   Reflect: What worked? Where did you lose certainty?

Boss Law #58: The person who practices influence daily never worries about income monthly.

ACTION BLUEPRINT: THE BOSS CLOSER'S SYSTEM

- Pick three common objections your clients have.
- Write a 1-sentence reframe for each.
- Practice your Boss Offer sentence in 3 tonal variations.
- Schedule a call or DM session within the next 24 hours.

Boss Law #59: Certainty is the highest currency in sales, spend it wisely.

JOURNAL PROMPT: THE VOICE OF CERTAINTY

- What does certainty sound like when you speak about your offer?
- Where do you still hesitate, and what belief must you strengthen to remove that hesitation forever?

THE ART OF FOLLOW-UP, UPSELLING WITHOUT SHAME, AND SCALING YOUR SALES RHYTHM

Boss Law #60: Follow-up isn't annoying, it's leadership with patience.

THURSDAY NIGHT: THE REAL SALE STARTS AFTER "NO"

The first time you hear "I'll think about it" isn't the end. It's the beginning of a decision-making process that most people abandon too early. The truth?

Deals are rarely won in the first conversation; they're closed in the follow-up rhythm. A "no" today is often just "not yet." Your job as a Boss is to hold a belief strong enough for both of you until the client catches up.

THE SAVAGE FOLLOW-UP RHYTHM

<u>Connect</u> → <u>Clarify</u> → <u>Close</u>

Follow-ups are not pestering, they're reminders of possibility. You're not chasing, you're guiding someone toward what they already want.

The 3-Touch System:

1. Follow-Up #1 (Day 1): Send genuine gratitude and keep it light. "Hey [Name], I really appreciated our chat. Here's the recap link we talked about."

2. Follow-Up #2 (Day 3): Add value without pressure. "I was thinking about your [problem]. Here's a quick insight that might help while you decide."

3. Follow-Up #3 (Day 7): Calm, confident close. "Totally respect where you're at. When you're ready, we'll build this together."

Boss Law #61: Follow-up turns forgotten conversations into found revenue.

The Psychology of Following Up Like a Boss

- Certainty transfers: When you believe in your offer, they feel it.
- Relevance reigns: Every message should add clarity or confidence.
- Silence means timing, not rejection: Most deals revive when they feel trust, not pressure.

"Persistence without pressure is the hallmark of a true closer."

THE 2X UPSELL SYSTEM

After you close one sale, the next is easier because you already have trust. Upselling isn't greed; it's guidance. You're helping clients continue their transformation.

Boss Law #62: The highest form of service is showing someone the next level once they've conquered the first.

Upselling Without Shame

The best upsells are natural extensions of your client's success.

If They Bought	Offer The Upgrade
Starter Coaching	6-week deep dive
Logo design	Full brand identity system
Fitness plan	90-day transformation
Copy audit	Complete launch strategy

Boss Tip: Always connect the upsell to momentum, not money.

"You've built great results so far. Let's keep this momentum going before it fades."

Case Study: The Momentum Upgrade

A small business owner bought a $99 audit. After seeing the gaps you revealed, they asked: "Can you just fix it?" You calmly positioned your $1,000 package as the logical next step. They said yes—not because of persuasion, but because of progress.

SCALING SALES WITH SYSTEMS

Boss Law #63: Consistency beats charisma, systems scale results.

To scale sales, you need rhythm, not randomness.

Your Daily Sales Dashboard:

Metric	Why It Matters
Leads Contacted	Measures Your Activity
Conversation Started	Reflects Engagement
Calls Booked	Tracks Commitment
Deals Closed	Show Conversion
Upsells Offered	Reveals Follow-Through

Track these weekly. Review every Friday. Adjust like a strategist, not an amateur.

Automation: The Invisible Assistant

You don't need a big team to scale; you need smart tools that multiply your time.

- Calendly for booking calls
- Notion or Google Sheets for tracking sales
- Zapier to connect forms and follow-ups
- Stripe or PayPal for instant payment links

Boss Law #64: Automation doesn't replace hustle, it amplifies it.

Delegation: Building Your Support Machine

Start small. Hire a virtual assistant or part-time admin once revenue allows. Outsource the busy work so you can stay focused on influence.

- Admin tasks → VA
- Design tweaks → Fiverr/Upwork
- Scheduling → Automated system

"Every hour you delegate is another hour you sell, lead, or build."

Batching: The Sales Athlete's Secret

You're not multitasking, you're managing momentum.

Task	Batch It
Dm Outreach	30 minutes, twice a week
Sales Calls	3-hour Thursday block
Follow-ups	Friday morning ritual

By grouping work, you create mental flow. Zero switching, zero burnout.

Boss Law #65: Time multiplies for those who manage attention like money.

Your 7-Day Sales Engine (Sample Routine)

Day	Focus
Monday	Prospecting + Outreach
Tuesday	Nurture Conversations
Wednesday	Sales Calls
Thursday	Upsells + New Offers
Friday	Review Dashboard + Referrals
Saturday	Rest + Reflect
Sunday	Plan Next Week's Visibility

Client Retention: The Hidden Empire

Your clients aren't one-time transactions; they're the seeds of your empire. Deliver value beyond expectations:

- Send a personalised thank-you video.
- Give them a bonus guide related to their purchase.
- Check in after 2 weeks, even if they didn't ask.

"Your reputation isn't built by what you sell, it's built by how you serve after the sale."

Boss Law #66: Referrals are the trust interest.

Referral Script Example

"I've really enjoyed working with you. Do you know one or two people who'd benefit from the same result we achieved together?"

Simple. Confident. Respectful.

Case Study: Referral Chain Reaction

One satisfied client introduced you to two others—each of those referred one more. Within 30 days, you had new clients and zero ad spend. That's the compounding effect of service excellence.

ACTION BLUEPRINT: THE SAVAGE SELLER'S ROUTINE

- Follow up with three cold leads and two warm prospects.
- Write one reframe for your most common objection.
- Track metrics in your Boss Dashboard.
- Schedule next week's visibility and follow-up blocks.
- Create one upsell path from your current offer.

Boss Law #67: Sales mastery is not about pressure; it's about precision.

JOURNAL PROMPT: SALES LEGACY

- "How can I serve so well that every client becomes my marketing?"
- "What system can I build today that will make tomorrow's sales automatic?"

END OF DAY REFLECTION

Thursday is not about chasing money; it's about proving leadership through service. You don't sell to survive anymore. You sell because you believe people deserve better, and you're the one who can deliver it.

Friday morning, the world meets the new version of you:

Confident. Consistent. Boss.

DAY 5
BOSS MODE –
DELIVER, UPSELL & SCALE

Boss Law #68: The first 24 hours define the next 24 weeks.

THE FRIDAY EVOLUTION: FROM HUSTLE TO OPERATION

Friday isn't victory-lap energy. It's operator energy—calm, calculated, controlled.

On Monday, you built belief. Tuesday, you weaponised your value. On Wednesday, you became visible. Thursday, you sold with certainty. Now, on Friday, you prove you belong here by delivering like a professional and scaling like a CEO. Bosses don't chase new money every day. They design systems that keep money moving while they sleep.

"The ultimate flex isn't freedom from work. It's freedom through systems."

THE DELIVERY MASTER SYSTEM
1. The 24-Hour Rule: Shock & Awe

The first 24 hours after a sale decide whether you'll be remembered as just another service or the best decision they ever made.

- Immediate Gratitude: Send a personalised thank-you within an hour. "Hey [Name], I'm genuinely excited to work with you. Here's what happens next."
- Clarity Checklist: Spell out what they can expect: Deliverables, milestones, and when the first update arrives.
- Quick Win: Deliver a tangible first outcome fast. A fitness coach sends a starter plan within 24 hours. A designer delivers a first-look preview. A consultant sends an "audit snapshot."

**Boss Law #69: Speed builds confidence.
Clarity keeps it.**

2. The Client Welcome Experience

Clients want reassurance that they've partnered with a professional. Create a Welcome Pack that covers:

Your process — What happens week by week.
How to communicate — Where and how you'll update them.
What success looks like — Define measurable wins early.

Include a branded PDF or Notion page with your logo, tone, and a "Meet Your Boss Process" section. It says: "This isn't my first project; this is my system."

3. Progress Over Perfection

A client's biggest fear is silence. Send short, high-frequency progress updates. Even "We're on track" maintains certainty.

- Weekly Update Template. Subject: Progress Update — [Client Name / Project Title]
- What we've completed
- What's in progress
- Next milestone
- Questions for you

Transparency creates retention, not marketing.

Boss Law #70: Clients don't leave when things slow down. They leave when they stop hearing from you.

4. The Client Dashboard

Treat every client like they're your only one, even when you're managing ten. A Client Dashboard (built in Notion, Airtable, or Sheets) tracks:

Client	Start Date	Deliverables	Progress %	Last Update	Next Milestone

Color-code it. Green = On track, Yellow = Check-in, Red = Urgent.

Small move, massive trust.

5. Boss Mindset: Delivery as Branding

Every interaction is marketing. Each deliverable, message, and update communicates your brand's promise.

"Brand is not a logo. It's the emotional aftertaste of every experience someone has with you."

Consistency = Credibility.

Professionalism = Proof.

Boss Law #71: Flawless delivery is the most powerful form of advertising.

THE CLIENT EXPERIENCE ECOSYSTEM
1. Build a System, Not a Sequence

An ecosystem keeps clients moving through a cycle of success:

<u>Onboard</u> → <u>Deliver</u> → <u>Celebrate</u> → <u>Upsell</u> → <u>Refer</u>

Each stage feeds the next. When clients finish, they already know what comes next because you've prepared them emotionally.

Example: After a 6-week coaching block, send a progress report that includes:

- What they've achieved
- Next-level goal suggestion
- Optional upgrade offer

You're leading. Not selling.

2. The Retention Flywheel

Retention = Revenue without pressure.

Action	Outcome
Check in bi-weekly	Keeps engagement alive
Celebrate small wins	Reinforces loyalty
Share insights	Adds ongoing value
Ask for feedback	Builds improvement loops

Boss Law #72: Retention is cheaper than reach, and more profitable than new acquisition.

3. The Renewal Trigger

Renewals happen naturally when clients can see their growth. Use visuals: screenshots, progress graphs, before-and-after comparisons.

At the end of each project, present a Milestone Summary Deck. Short, clean, impressive.

End with: "Here's what we've built together so far—and what we can build next."

You've just positioned the upsell without selling.

4. When Problems Arise: Lead, Don't React

Mistakes happen. Bosses own them early.

- Acknowledge fast and clearly.
- Offer a solution before the client asks.
- Follow up to ensure trust is restored.

Boss Law #73: Integrity under pressure
builds authority under prosperity.

5. Case Study: From Player to Provider

A former athlete turned entrepreneur used his experience running training sessions to build a client process. Each new academy student received a custom plan within 24 hours, weekly video feedback, and monthly progress dashboards.

Word of mouth doubled his enrolments in three months. No ads, no sales calls, just systemised delivery. That's Boss Mode in action: Deliver excellence so loudly the world hears about it for you.

6. Action Blueprint: The Client Experience Audit

Before you scale, audit your delivery:

Question	If No → Fix This
Do I communicate the next steps clearly?	Create a welcome template
Do clients get early wins?	Add a quick win deliverable
Do I follow up weekly?	Schedule automated check-ins
Do I track progress visually?	Build a client dashboard
Do I ask for feedback monthly?	Add a feedback form

Perform this audit every Friday before logging off. That's how you end the week like a Boss.

JOURNAL PROMPT
- "Where can I add 10% more clarity or speed to what I deliver next week?"
- "How can I make my clients feel like partners, not purchases?"

You've built the machine. Now you'll learn to fuel it forever.

UPSCALING, AUTOMATION & THE BOSS MANIFESTO

Boss Law #74: You can't scale chaos;
you can only automate clarity.

THE 2X UPSELL SYSTEM: MULTIPLYING VALUE WITHOUT PRESSURE

Sales don't stop when the invoice clears. They evolve. Upselling isn't about squeezing more money; it's about unlocking deeper transformation for the people you already serve.

You've already earned their trust. Now you simply extend the journey.

1. The Momentum-Based Upsell
Right after delivery, the client feels empowered. That's the moment momentum is highest, and when Bosses strike with empathy, not aggression.

Instead of saying, "Would you like to buy more?"

You ask: "Would you like to go further?"

That one word shift—further—reframes the upsell as growth, not greed.

2. The Ladder Framework

Tier	Offer Type	Outcome
$100	Starter ot trial	Test confidence & build trust
$500	Core transformation	Real measurable win
$5000	Premium elite tier	Life or business shift

This ladder ensures every offer naturally leads to the next. If your lowest tier converts, your higher ones become a foregone conclusion.

Boss Law #75: You don't need new clients every week. You need to serve your current ones at the highest level.

3. The Psychological Trigger of Continuation

Clients fear regression more than investment. That's your leverage. "You've built this momentum, the worst thing now is to lose it. Let's keep it compounding."

Reinforce that progress is a privilege. People pay to keep winning.

AUTOMATION: BUYING BACK YOUR TIME

Boss Law #76: Automation doesn't make you less human. It lets you spend your humanity where it matters.

When you automate right, clients feel more supported, not less.

1. Build the Invisible Assistant
- Calendly or TidyCal: Bookings without back-and-forths.
- Zapier or Make: Automatically send client welcome emails and update progress sheets.

- Notion/ClickUp: Manage clients, notes, and deliverables in one dashboard.
- Stripe or PayPal Links: No "send me your details". Just payment, instant confirmation, automated.

Automation gives you more time to sell, lead, and serve.

2. Create the Boss Flow

A simple 5-step pipeline that runs daily:

Lead → Call → Sale → Delivery → Follow-Up → Upsell

Each step has one automation:

Stage	Automation
Lead Capture	Form → CRM
Call Booking	Calendly integration
Sale	Stripe link + invoice email
Delivery	Notion project auto-create
Follow up	Three day automated email

You now run like an agency, even if you're solo.

3. Delegate What Doesn't Require You

Task	Delegate to
Scheduling & Admin	Virtual Assistant
Basic Design	Freelancer (fiverr, upwork)
Data Entry	VA or Automation
Research	Junior Assistant

Your job is sales, systems, and strategy. Everything else gets delegated or automated.

"A true Boss focuses on what multiplies money, not what maintains it."

SCALING SYSTEMS: FROM SOLO TO STRUCTURE

1. The 30-Day Scale Model

You don't need to scale forever, just 30 focused days of clarity.

Week	Focus
1.	Audit your delivery + setup automations
2.	Create a second offer or bundle
3.	Hire part-time help (VA or editor)
4.	Build weekly recurring routines

Boss Law #77: Scale begins the moment
you stop improvising.

2. Building a Micro-Team

Start with three core functions:

- Operations: Handles delivery logistics.
- Communications: Handles messaging & updates.
- Growth: Handles content, outreach, or visibility.

Even if it's just you, define these roles. Operate like a company before you can afford one, because that's how you earn one.

3. The CEO Routine

A CEO doesn't wake up asking "What should I do today?" They know exactly where they are in the system.

Morning: Lead generation review.
Midday: Client updates or team sync.
Evening: Metrics + journal reflection.

Three hours a day of focused action will outperform ten hours of chaos.

Boss Law #78: Time doesn't make you successful, clarity does.

CLIENT RETENTION: THE MULTIPLIER EFFECT

Every satisfied client becomes a marketing asset.

1. Referral Loops

End every project with a straightforward script: "Do you know anyone else who'd benefit from what we just achieved?"

Add a small incentive—a bonus session, discount, or credit. This converts gratitude into growth.

2. Testimonials: The Modern Word-of-Mouth

Ask for testimonials while emotions are high.

Provide an easy template: "Before working with me, I was [problem]. After [specific action], I achieved [result]."

Polish and post. That's your new inbound engine.

Boss Law #79: The results you deliver sell harder than any ad.

3. The 90-Day Review

At the end of every quarter, review every client journey.

Ask:
- Did I communicate clearly?
- Did I deliver early?
- Did I provide growth pathways?

Small improvements here double retention and referrals.

Friday ends with reflection, not exhaustion. You've built a system, a mindset, and a brand of consistency. Now you transition from executor to architect. You are not chasing money anymore. You are designing a machine that prints proof of your discipline.

THE FIVE BOSS COMMANDMENTS

1. Decide daily. The world moves for those who commit.
2. Communicate clearly. Confusion kills conversions.
3. Deliver fast. Momentum creates belief.
4. Lead with value. Every message builds your brand.
5. Repeat with discipline. Consistency compounds forever.

THE WEEKLY BOSS ROUTINE

Day	Focus
Monday	Vision & Planning
Tuesday	Offer Development
Wednesday	Visibility
Thursday	Sales & Follow-Up
Friday	Delivery & Reflection
Saturday	Rest
Sunday	Strategy Reset

Boss Law #80: Momentum loves routine.

JOURNAL PROMPT: THE BOSS LEGACY

- "What will my clients, my peers, and my results say about how I operated?"

- "Where can I build systems so strong that my success no longer depends on mood or motivation?"

You started this week as a dreamer. You're ending it as an operator.

You've proven to yourself that clarity + execution = transformation. Now repeat the process until it becomes your lifestyle.

**Boss Law #81: You don't need permission.
You just need repetition.**

LEADERSHIP, LEGACY & LONG-TERM GROWTH

**Boss Law #82: Leaders don't manage time.
They design environments that multiply it.**

THE EVOLUTION: FROM OPERATOR TO ARCHITECT

Friday evening. The world slows down. The hustlers celebrate the weekend. The Boss prepares for the next era. All week, you've been executing. But mastery begins when you start designing and shaping systems that win without your constant touch.

This is where momentum becomes infrastructure. You are no longer in the game to survive. You are here to build a machine that sustains itself, scales itself, and inspires others to do the same.

THE THREE PHASES OF LEADERSHIP GROWTH

1. Operator — driven by adrenaline and action.
2. Architect — driven by design and delegation.
3. Authority — driven by vision and impact.

Bosses move through these stages consciously.

The Operator builds results.

The Architect builds systems.

The Authority builds movements.

"Freedom doesn't come from escaping work. It comes from engineering work that runs without you."

BUILDING THE REPUTATION FLYWHEEL

Boss Law #83: Authority is built in public by those who serve privately with excellence.

Your reputation is now your strongest form of leverage. The more consistent your results, the more attention compounds.

The 4 Pillars of Reputation

Pillar	Definition	Execution
Credibility	Proof you deliver	Case studies + client wins
Consistency	Proof you show up	Weekly content + updates
Connection	Proof you care	Community engagement
Contribution	Proof you grow others	Mentorship + education

Together, these create an unstoppable feedback loop:

Deliver → Document → Display → Dominate

Each loop increases visibility without needing ads or noise.

Authority Without Arrogance

Bosses don't brag; they broadcast results through stories and education. Replace "look at me" with "look at what's possible." This shift builds trust and followers who buy for transformation, not trend.

MONEY MASTERY: THE FINANCIAL FOUNDATION

Boss Law #84: Cashflow clarity = Decision freedom.

Money is no longer chaos; it's data. And data tells you where freedom hides.

The Boss Financial Blueprint

Category	Purpose	Allocation
Delivery (60%)	Operation + tools	Ensure client excellence
Reinvestment (30%)	Growth + ads + education	Build assets & skills
Lifestyle (10%)	Reward + balance	Celebrate without chaos

Set up a separate business account. Automate transfers for tax and savings.

Create a weekly Cashflow Check-In ritual every Friday afternoon, 10 minutes that keep you from ever feeling broke again.

Profit Over Revenue

You don't need a $1 million brand. You need a profitable one.

Profit is peace. Profit is longevity.

"A business that looks rich and runs poor is just a brand on life support."

PERSONAL LEADERSHIP & TEAM CULTURE

Boss Law #85: The culture you build will eventually build you.

Leadership is not about control. It's about clarity.

Whether you're a solo entrepreneur or leading a team, the standard you set in your behavior becomes the standard others follow.

The 5 Leadership Disciplines

1. Be early. Respect time as you expect others to.
2. Communicate with clarity, not urgency.
3. Solve in private, praise in public.
4. Protect your team's energy like your own.
5. Teach more than you tell.

When you operate with these principles, you build an ecosystem of trust that scales faster than ads.

Creating a Micro-Culture

Even if you only work with freelancers or assistants, build a culture:

- Monday Wins: Quick check-ins on what worked.
- Mid-Week Sync: Short alignment call.
- Friday Wrap-Up: Celebrate progress openly.

Culture creates consistency. Consistency creates momentum.

HEALTH & HIGH PERFORMANCE

**Boss Law #86: Discipline is the bridge
between growth and longevity.**

You can't lead with burnout. Peak performance isn't about grind, it's about precision.

The Boss Performance Pyramid

Layer	Focus	Outcome
Foundation	Sleep + Nutrition	Sustained energy
Core	Movement + Mindset	Resilience
Apex	Focus + Flow	Creative dominance

Daily Non-Negotiables
- 30 minutes of movement each day.
- 1 hour deep work block, no notifications.
- 10 min gratitude or reflection.

You can't scale a broken system, especially if that system is you.

THE LEGACY LAYER

**Boss Law #87: Your legacy is written
in systems, not speeches.**

Legacy isn't what you leave behind. It's what you build that keeps working when you step back.

- Document your systems so others can replicate them.
- Teach what you've learned through mentorship, content, or courses.
- Build community. People who build each other up under your vision.

When your systems start serving others, you move from entrepreneur to leader of leaders.

"Your real ROI is how many people grow because you didn't quit."

BOSS CHALLENGE

Boss Law #88: Teaching multiplies mastery.

Your final challenge isn't to read, it's to repeat and reinforce.

30-Day Boss Mode Expansion

Week	Objective
1.	Repeat the 5-Day cycle
2.	Build one new automation
3.	Teach one lesson to someone else
4.	Review metrics + adjust your system

Every cycle creates momentum. Every iteration builds identity.

FINAL REFLECTION: THE BOSS WITHIN

Friday night, you're not just finishing a challenge. You're completing a transformation. You've turned discipline into design. Fear into focus. Uncertainty into systems. The world will still spin the same on Monday, but you won't.

Boss Law #89: You didn't just survive the week. You rewired who you are.

"The Boss life isn't about freedom from work, it's about mastery of self."

THE MARKETING BOSS PLAYBOOK

THE PSYCHOLOGY OF MAGNETIC MARKETING

Boss Law #90: Marketing is not about being seen, it's about being remembered.

THE ATTENTION ARENA

Picture this: It's Monday morning. You unlock your phone, and within 60 seconds, you're hit with over three thousand competing messages. Every brand, expert, and wannabe influencer is shouting: "Look at me!" Welcome to the Attention Arena, the modern battlefield of influence.

Only one kind of player wins here: The one who understands emotion, not just information. Most marketers chase algorithms. Bosses master human behavior.

The truth is simple: Attention is no longer earned by volume; it's earned by resonance. In this game, facts don't sell. Feelings do. The smartest brand doesn't always win. The most emotionally relevant one does.

EMOTION VS LOGIC: THE BUYING BATTLE

Every buying decision passes through two gates:

1. The Heart Gate (Emotion): "Do I feel something?"
2. The Head Gate (Logic): "Can I justify it?"

The order never changes. Emotion decides. Logic defends. Think back to your last premium purchase—a watch, a mentorship, a training kit. You didn't just buy the item. You bought the feeling of becoming the person who owns it. Boss marketers don't manipulate emotion; they guide it with precision.

Boss Law #91: People buy emotion and justify with logic.

THE PAIN → POSSIBILITY → PROOF → PATH CYCLE

This is your Magnetic Marketing Sequence, the timeless backbone of trust and persuasion.

1. Pain: Expose the truth.
   Surface the frustration your audience already feels.
   "You've been posting for months, but nobody's buying. Not because your product is bad, but because your message isn't clear."

2. Possibility: Offer the vision.
   Paint a picture of what their life could look like.
   "Imagine building a brand that attracts opportunities while you sleep."

3. Proof: Provide credibility.
   Results, screenshots, transformations—proof that the promise works.
   "Here's how we helped 30 clients 10x engagement with one storytelling tweak."

4. Path: Give the next step.
   Make it simple and low friction.
   "Download the 5-step template and start today."

Each phase flows like a natural conversation, not a hard pitch.

Each step builds permission, not pressure.

PSYCHOLOGY PYRAMID: THE FOUR EMOTIONAL DRIVERS OF DECISION

1. STATUS: "Will this make me feel significant?"
   People buy elevation, not things. Example: A high-performance football academy doesn't just sell training—it sells transformation from player to leader. It markets identity, not drills.

2. SAFETY: "Can I trust you?"
   People buy from those who feel safe, predictable, and honest. Example: A consulting service that guarantees clarity in 30 minutes gives clients certainty—the rarest currency in business.

3. BELONGING: "Do people like me do this?"
   Humans are tribal. A community of like-minded individuals validates identity. Example: A mentorship that connects entrepreneurs with peers builds instant trust through shared ambition.

4. TRANSFORMATION: "Will this make me better?"
   At the core, buyers crave growth. Example: A Boss-level online training or fitness plan doesn't just promise weight loss, it delivers self-mastery.

Great brands hit all four emotional drivers, but elite ones lead with one—the Primary Emotional Trigger that defines their essence.

STORYTELLING AS THE GATEWAY TO TRUST

Logic informs.

Story transforms.

Stories bypass resistance because they let your audience see themselves in the journey. A Boss marketer uses micro-stories, real moments that create emotion and teach a principle. They act as the emotional bridge between authority and authenticity.

Types of micro-stories:
- Before-and-after transformations
- Lessons learned from failure
- Mini client wins and milestones

Each one humanises you, proving your expertise without bragging.

Example (Service-Based):

"When I first transitioned from football into business, I carried the same discipline—training, repetition, constant analysis. But the real win came when I learned how to communicate that discipline to clients. When I shifted my message from 'what I do' to 'why it matters,' my academy doubled its inquiries in 30 days. It wasn't luck, it was alignment."

Example (Product-Based):

"When an emerging designer launched a minimalist clothing line, they knew they weren't just selling fabric; they were selling identity. Every stitch, cut, and design carried a message: Discipline is luxury.

The brand's story wasn't about trends or hype. It was about transformation. Turning the mindset of ambition into something you could wear. Their campaign slogan said it all: 'For those who move different.' Each hoodie, jacket, and t-shirt represented a mentality—calm confidence, quiet power, relentless pursuit.

They weren't marketing apparel. They were marketing the lifestyle of earned respect. Within weeks, their online store gained traction not because of discounts or gimmicks, but because people didn't just want the clothes. They wanted to represent the standard the brand stood for."

Stories are the gateway to loyalty. They convert faster than features and build emotional equity you can't buy with ads.

Boss Law #92: Facts tell. Stories sell.

INVISIBLE FUNNEL FLOW

Traditional funnels try to trap people. Bosses funnel guide them through curiosity, trust, and value.

The new funnel:

<u>Trust</u> → <u>Interest</u> → <u>Desire</u> → <u>Decision</u>

Every piece of content becomes a natural step in this flow:
- A personal story sparks Trust
- A valuable insight builds Interest
- A client result creates Desire
- A direct call to action invites a Decision

You don't push people down a funnel; you walk beside them through one.

You've just learned the real engine behind marketing that sticks:
- Emotion drives attention.
- Story drives connection.
- Clarity drives conversion.

Emotion is your accelerator. Logic is your brake.

Great marketing knows when to use both.

In the next section, we'll turn this psychology into a repeatable system that generates trust and sales automatically, without acting like a salesperson.

BUILDING EMOTIONAL SYSTEMS FOR INFLUENCE

Boss Law #93: Emotion creates attention, systems sustain it.

THE SHIFT FROM INSTINCT TO INFRASTRUCTURE

Most people market like gamblers, throwing posts into the void and hoping one hits. Bosses don't gamble. They engineer. They turn what once felt like intuition into a repeatable, measurable process. Magnetic marketing is not a lucky spark. It's a structure of emotion built to fire consistently. And when you install that structure, visibility stops being a chase and becomes a rhythm.

THE EMOTIONAL ARCHITECTURE FRAMEWORK

Think of emotion as electricity. If you don't channel it through the correct wiring, it burns out fast.

Your framework has three layers:
1. Trigger: What grabs attention (emotion)
2. Anchor: What holds attention (story)
3. Action: What transfers attention into momentum (offer)

Each post, campaign, or conversation should flow through this invisible sequence.

It's not about being loud, it's about being felt.

Example:
- Trigger → "Most entrepreneurs fail because they sell effort, not results."
- Anchor → Story about wasted hours before learning the Boss Offer Formula.

- Action → "Here's how to design your first results-based offer in 24 hours."

That flow builds trust and curiosity simultaneously.

THE RESONANCE LOOP

Boss Law #94: Repetition isn't redundancy when your message evolves.

The average person needs 7–12 touchpoints to trust a new brand. But here's the truth: People don't get bored with your message; they get bored with how you say it. The Resonance Loop is the rhythm of message reinforcement:

Stage	Purpose	Example
1.	Reveal	Share a personal story about early struggles.
2.	Reinforce	Teach a short concept that supports that story.
3.	Reframe	Update the same lesson from a new perspective (client win, quote, insight)
4.	Remind	Summarise and invite the audience to act.

One idea, recycled through these four angles, becomes a brand pillar. It keeps your narrative fresh without diluting your identity.

THE ATTENTION ECOSYSTEM

Attention is a living organism. It must be fed consistently but never force-fed. Your Attention Ecosystem is made up of three energy zones:

- Core Content: Long-form, high-value posts, videos, or newsletters that position you as the expert.

- Conversation Content: Stories, replies, and comments that humanise your brand.
- Conversion Content: Offers and invitations that turn trust into transactions.

**Boss Law #95: If your ecosystem dies,
your income follows.**

Bosses manage their ecosystem like a gym routine:
- Core = training days
- Conversation = recovery days
- Conversion = competition day

They all serve the same body, your business.

THE 3-TOUCH INFLUENCE MODEL

Before someone buys from you, they go through three invisible checkpoints:

1. Exposure Touch – They notice you.
2. Emotional Touch – They feel understood by you.
3. Evidence Touch – They see that what you do works.

Missing any of these steps means lost sales.

The best marketers design content calendars that deliberately rotate through all three.

Example weekly flow:
- Monday → Story post (Emotional Touch)
- Wednesday → Educational post (Evidence Touch)
- Friday → Offer + CTA (Exposure Touch through reach content)

THE TRUST ENGINE

Trust is built in micro-moments. Every comment, message, and email is a piece of data that either compounds or decays that trust.

To build your Trust Engine, follow the "3 C Protocol":
1. Clarity – Always state what you do in under one sentence.
2. Consistency – Keep tone and visuals aligned.
3. Competence – Show results; never fake them.

> Boss Law #96: Trust is the currency that makes every other system work.

CASE STUDY: THE CONSISTENCY COMPANY

A new online fitness brand spent six months posting occasionally, with zero momentum. When they applied the Attention Ecosystem model:

- They assigned each weekday a clear emotional goal.
- They repurposed old posts using the Resonance Loop.
- They replaced "buy now" CTAs with "start your transformation today."

Result: Engagement grew 80%, inbound DMs tripled, and conversions doubled without a single ad. Their strategy didn't change; their system did.

THE EMOTIONAL AUTOMATION BLUEPRINT

Automation isn't cold. It's commitment at scale. Your automation system should never sound robotic; it should amplify empathy.

1. Capture Emotion → Use lead magnets or DM scripts that promise a feeling, not a file.
2. Nurture Trust → Send story-based follow-ups that mirror your audience's pain.
3. Guide Decision → Introduce offers as the natural next step in their journey.

Each message in your automation should feel like it was written that morning, just for them.

THE EMOTIONAL SYSTEM MAP

<u>Heart</u> → <u>Emotion</u> → <u>Story</u> → <u>System</u> → <u>Trust</u> → <u>Sale</u> → <u>Referral</u> → <u>Back to Heart</u>

This shows the flywheel effect of emotional systems: One buyer becomes your next marketer.

THE MIRROR METHOD

Bosses audit their marketing monthly using this three-question mirror:

1. Is my message still emotionally charged?
2. Is my content still strategically aligned?
3. Is my audience still growing through my work?

If the answer to any is "no," recalibrate. Not by changing your goal, but by strengthening your rhythm.

THE SYSTEMISATION SCORECARD

Use this quick diagnostic to measure the strength of your marketing system:

Area	Rating (1-10)	Fix or Focus
Message Clarity		
Story Consistency		
Audience Resonance		
Offer Conversion		
Retention / Referrals		

Total 40–50 = Boss Level.

Below 30 = you're running on hustle, not systems.

ACTION BLUEPRINT: BUILD YOUR SYSTEM

- Identify your core emotional trigger, what your brand stands for emotionally.
- Create three message pillars around that trigger.
- Design your Resonance Loop calendar.
- Automate trust through story-based email sequences.
- Review metrics weekly; adjust monthly.

When you complete this, marketing becomes muscle memory.

JOURNAL PROMPT:

- "Where am I still relying on luck instead of the system?"
- "What emotion does my audience associate with my brand, and is it the one I intended?"
- Write the answers and build your next 90-day rhythm from them.

Emotion begins the conversation. Systems continue it. When they merge, your marketing becomes inevitable. Not loud, not forced, but magnetic.

> **Boss Law #97: Emotion makes you visible.**
> **Systems make you unforgettable.**

POSITIONING: BECOMING UNCOPYABLE

> **Boss Law #98: You don't compete**
> **when you define the game.**

THE DEATH OF COMPETITION

Competition is the comfort zone of the average. When everyone is fighting to be "better," the true Boss asks, "What can I do that makes me the only?"

Being better is subjective. Being different is unforgettable. Positioning is the invisible moat that protects empires. The unspoken reason people choose you over everyone else, even when others are louder, cheaper, or newer.

The world doesn't pay the most to the hardest worker. It pays the most to the clearest leader.

THE POWER OF PERCEPTION

Perception = Reality × Repetition.

People don't see the full truth. They see the version of it you repeat with consistency. A mediocre brand positioned as a movement will outperform a genius positioned as a commodity. The marketplace rewards clarity, not complexity.

You are either seen as:
- A specialist solving a mission-critical problem, or
- A generalist solving nothing in particular.

In the digital age, generalists get ignored. Specialists get paid.

**Boss Law #99: The riches are in precision,
not variety.**

THE 1 PROBLEM → 1 PROMISE → 1 PERSON MODEL

This is how modern authority is built. Every magnetic brand can articulate three things in one breath:

1. One Problem:
   "My audience is stuck because…"
   Example: Small fitness coaches can't stand out in a flooded market.

2. One Promise:
   "I help them achieve…"
   Example: A recognisable brand that attracts clients without paid ads.

3. One Person:
"This is for…"
Example: Ambitious fitness entrepreneurs ready to go full-time.

You do not need a massive audience. You need a focused message that sounds like it was written for one person only. When you master this, you stop chasing opportunities. They start chasing you.

THE BOSS POSITIONING FRAMEWORK

<u>Identity</u> → <u>Promise</u> → <u>Process</u> → <u>Proof</u> → <u>Personality</u>

- IDENTITY – Who you are.
  Your brand essence, your belief system, your "why." If you disappeared tomorrow, what would your audience lose?

- PROMISE – What you deliver.
  Not features. Not hours. Transformation. What tangible outcome do you guarantee?

- PROCESS – How you get results.
  Your proprietary method, your unique path. The clearer your framework, the higher your perceived authority.

- PROOF – Why you're trusted.
  Testimonials, screenshots, wins, credibility triggers. In the social era, proof is public currency.

- PERSONALITY – Why you're loved.
  The flavor that can't be duplicated—tone, humor, visuals, rhythm. Without personality, you're just a PDF with a logo. When these five align, your brand becomes uncopyable. Competitors can steal your ideas, but never your identity.

Real-World Example: The Specialist Coach

A strength coach was losing clients to low-price trainers. Instead of offering "fitness plans," he repositioned:

"I help former athletes rebuild peak performance in 90 days—without pain, pills, or plateaus."

He didn't change his skills. He changed the lens. By defining one person and one promise, he turned confusion into conviction. Within months, he tripled revenue, not by scaling ads, but by scaling clarity.

Boss Law #100: Clarity outperforms confidence.

People buy the brand that explains their problem better than they can.

THE POSITIONING PYRAMID

- Top – Promise
- Middle – Process + Proof
- Base – Identity + Personality

Most brands start at the top, trying to sell the promise before building the base. A true Boss builds from the ground up: purpose first, perception second, profit third.

FROM INVISIBLE TO INEVITABLE

When positioning clicks, something shifts. People start describing you in ways you never told them to.

They say: "You're the one who does X," or "I thought of you when I saw this."

That's the sign your story has become their shorthand. A Boss doesn't chase virality; they build mental real estate. They own one word, one feeling, one transformation in the mind of their market.

- Nike → Performance
- Apple → Innovation
- Tesla → Rebellion
- You → ?

Define it, and everything else will orbit around it.

STORY AS STRATEGY

Your story is not your resume. It's the reason your audience believes you can lead them. The right brand story contains three beats:

1. The Gap — where you started.
2. The Shift — what you discovered.
3. The Gift — how you now help others cross that same bridge.

Keep it emotional but functional.

Every story should either build belief, reduce doubt, or reinforce identity.

Case Study — Product Brand: The Designer Collective

A young designer launched a clothing label but couldn't scale up sales. Instead of selling "shirts," she reframed her message:

"We design statement pieces for builders—the 1% who create, not consume."

Each item carried a story stitched inside the tag. A quote about ambition, persistence, or resilience. Customers didn't just wear the product; they wore identity. The brand stopped being apparel. It became armor.

That's the essence of positioning, when your product becomes a mirror for the buyer's self-image.

Boss Law #101: Sell the transformation,
not the transaction.

BECOMING UNCOPYABLE: THE REFLECTION

- What problem do you own that no one else solves quite like you?
- What promise makes your audience believe change is possible?
- What process gives them confidence that you can deliver?
- What proof cements trust before you ever speak to them?
- What personality makes them remember you when you're not posting?

Answer these and you'll find your Uncopyable Brand Statement—your one-sentence summary of why you exist in your market.

Example: "I help ambitious creators turn their knowledge into scalable empires through brand clarity and magnetic content."

Short. Clear. Powerful.

CLOSING: THE BOSS MINDSET OF POSITIONING

Positioning isn't what you say about yourself. It's what your audience whispers when you're not in the room. A Boss doesn't fight for space. They create it. They don't copy strategies. They define categories.

Boss Law #102: Be so defined that imitation
looks like confusion.

In the next section, we'll transform this clarity into conversion, because once your position is set, every word, post, and offer must reinforce it.

CONTENT THAT CONVERTS

Boss Law #103: Content isn't about noise,
it's about narrative.

THE AGE OF INFINITE VOICES

Every scroll, every post, every podcast… someone is speaking.

The online world is louder than ever, and yet 99% of creators are invisible. The difference between the unknown and the unforgettable isn't followers—it's framework.

Boss-level marketers don't post randomly. They design content that converts emotion into engagement and engagement into income.

If the Psychology of Magnetic Marketing is your foundation, this is the execution. Here's where you turn insight into impact. With words, visuals, and consistency so sharp they cut through the noise.

THE 4 PILLARS OF CONTENT THAT CONVERTS

Every high-authority personal brand—whether coach, designer, or entrepreneur—is built on four unshakable pillars.

1. Value / Education: Teach Them Something They Can Use Today

> Boss Law #104: Teach before you pitch.
> Authority is earned through value.

Education-driven content positions you as the trusted expert. But most creators make one of two mistakes:

1. They teach too broadly ("5 generic tips for success").
2. They overwhelm ("everything I know in one post").

The Boss approach?

Deliver one sharp insight per piece. Leave them smarter, not stuffed.

Example (Coaching Offer): "Everyone says you need more discipline. Wrong. You need fewer decisions. Set one non-negotiable for the day, and the rest becomes automatic."

Example (Clothing Brand): "Fast fashion sells you trends. We sell you identity. One piece, made to last—so your style doesn't expire."

Template:

Hook: Call out the pain or misconception.

Truth: Teach a single insight.

Payoff: Show the result or shift.

CTA: Invite engagement or lead magnet.

2. Story / Relatability: Build Trust with Truth

Boss Law #105: Authenticity scales faster than algorithms.

Storytelling is your emotional bridge. It's where people connect to you, the human behind the value. You don't need trauma or drama. You need truth. Moments that show evolution, clarity, or conviction.

Example (Coach): "I didn't go viral. I went consistent. Thirty days of showing up online built me more clients than 2 years of hoping someone noticed."

Example (Clothing Brand): "Our first samples arrived wrong. Wrong fabric, wrong fit. But they represented something right—our refusal to compromise. Every failed prototype was a lesson in standards."

Use these micro-stories to show resilience, lessons, and transformation.

Each one is a trust deposit.

3. Proof / Results: Turn Trust Into Belief

Boss Law #106: Proof is the oxygen of persuasion.

You can't just say it works. You must show it.

There are three kinds of proof:
1. Social Proof: Testimonials, screenshots, user reviews.
2. Personal Proof: Your own transformations, behind-the-scenes moments.
3. Philosophical Proof: Your guiding principles, explained with logic and conviction.

Example (Mentor): "I helped 15 entrepreneurs launch offers that earned $50K+ collectively in 60 days—not through ads, but with this 3-step system."

Example (Clothing Brand): "When customers wear our designs, they tell us it's not about fashion—it's about finally feeling like themselves."

Visual Idea: A minimalist "Before / After" content mockup showing a brand's client journey or transformation story. Proof-driven content makes invisible trust visible.

4. CTA / Direct Offer: Tell Them What To Do Next

Boss Law #107: A clear call to action isn't salesy, it's leadership.

You've earned attention. Don't let it fade. Your audience wants direction, clarity beats cleverness every time. Think of your CTA as the bridge from curiosity to commitment.

Example CTAs:
- "DM 'START' if you're ready to build your first offer this week."
- "Comment 'STYLE' and I'll send you our limited drop preview."
- "Tap the link and download the 7-step visibility planner."

CTA Framework (The 3 Cs):
1. Clarity: Tell them exactly what to do.
2. Context: Tell them why.
3. Confidence: Assume they'll act.

THE 100% CONTENT FORMULA

The secret to scaling visibility and revenue simultaneously is not "posting more." It's posting smarter; every post should serve a business function. Here's the formula used by elite brands and solopreneurs:

1. 60% Authority Content: Teach, share frameworks, show expertise.
2. 20% Connection Content: Humanise. Show personality, mission, and beliefs.
3. 10% Proof Content: Show wins, feedback, and transformations.
4. 10% Offer Content: Direct promotions, launches, or CTAs.

When your content portfolio balances like this, you build omnipresence and credibility simultaneously.

VIDEO DOMINATION FRAMEWORK

If your written words build trust, your voice and face build conviction. Short-form video is the new elevator pitch, and Bosses master it.

Structure for 30–45 second Reels or TikToks:

HOOK (0–3s): Start with a pattern interrupt—something that makes people stop scrolling. "You're not broke. You're just invisible."

INSIGHT (4–15s): Deliver one bold truth. "You don't need more followers—you need a better offer. The algorithm isn't broken. Your clarity is."

VALUE (16–30s): Teach one applicable step. "Fix your bio. One sentence: 'I help X achieve Y in Z days.' That's it."

CTA (31–45s): End with a directive. "Save this, implement it, and DM me when it works."

Stay consistent, not creative.

CONTENT AS A SYSTEM: THE REPURPOSING LOOP

Boss marketers never create once. They multiply once. Here's how one idea becomes a month of content:

Original Idea	Format 1	Format 2	Format 3	Format 4
"How to craft your first offer"	Reel	Carousel	Tweet	Email
"Why 90% fail in business"	Mini rant video	Quote post	Podcast clip	Blog
"The Boss Morning Routine"	Story highlight	Infographic	Short post	Youtube short

This system transforms one deep concept into four audience touchpoints, without burnout or creative blocks.

Boss Law #108: Create once, distribute infinitely.

REFLECTION

You now know how to build content that does what most people only dream of: Attract, engage, and convert without ads, gimmicks, or burnout. Your content is no longer just marketing. It's a sales team, brand identity, and trust machine that works even while you sleep.

THE BOSS CONTENT SYSTEM: WEEKLY EXECUTION BLUEPRINT

Boss Law #109: Consistency builds authority. Precision builds legacy.

OVERVIEW

You don't need to post fifty times a day. You need a system that compounds. The Boss Content System turns one idea into seven days of authority, connection, and conversion. Each day has a dominant purpose, one pillar focus, and one execution format. Follow this blueprint, and you'll build omnipresence without burnout.

VISUAL MAP: WEEKLY CONTENT FLOW

Day	Focus Pillar	Objective	Format	Example (Coaching)	Example (Product Brand)
Monday	Value / Education	Teach one core Principle	Carousel / Short Post	"How to find your first client without ads"	Why premium cotton lasts longer, and it saves you money"
Tuesday	Story / Relatability	Build human connection	Story Post / Reel	"The first time I nearly quit, and what I learned"	"The chaos behind our first failed photo shoot"
Wednesday	Proof / Results	Show credibility & transformation	Testimonial / Screenshot / Story	"3 clients launched this week using the 2-step offer system"	"Customer photo: Wore this shirt 15 times and it still looks brand new"
Thursday	CTA / Direct Offer	Convert attention into action	Post / Reel / Email	"DM 'START' if you want to validate your offer this week"	"Our limited collection drops tonight, comment 'READY' for early access."
Friday	Value + Story	Deep insight with personal twist	Long-form post / Email	"The mindset shift that made me consistent online"	"Why we chose timeless designs over trends"
Saturday	Community & Engagement	Spark conversation / gather feedback	Pool / Q&A / Story	"What's your #1 struggle in growing your brand?"	"Which design should we drop next?"
Sunday	Reflection & Reset	Reinforce the message & preview next week	Quote / Behind the scenes	"One week done, remember: visibility beats, perfection"	"How we plan our weekly production - "the way"

The Flow Explained

MONDAY: EDUCATE WITH AUTHORITY

Set the tone. Start the week by teaching something actionable. This builds your credibility early and positions you as the go-to expert.

Boss Tip: Keep the first post of the week tactical, something your audience can do today.

People remember teachers, not talkers.

TUESDAY: HUMANISE YOUR BRAND

Now that you've earned attention, earn a connection. Share a lesson, a story, or a behind-the-scenes insight that shows you're real. Not robotic.

> Boss Law #110: People don't buy perfect;
> they purchase progress.

WEDNESDAY: DEMONSTRATE RESULTS

Midweek is for proof. This is where you move from authority to trust. Show wins. Share testimonials. Reveal numbers. Don't just say it works, show them why it matters.

Boss Example: Instead of "Client success!", write: "Grace applied one clarity exercise and booked her first $500 client within 72 hours."

THURSDAY: PITCH WITH POWER

Every week needs a CTA day; this is where you lead. Tell your audience exactly how to take the next step with you.

Use a soft CTA ("DM 'INFO'") or a hard CTA ("Join before midnight"). Both build the muscle of confidence, the foundation of leadership.

Boss Law #111: Sales is service when it solves a real problem.

FRIDAY: VALUE + STORY

This is your most emotional day. End strong, tie logic and inspiration together. Share something reflective, but still practical. This post connects your why to your how.

Example (Coach): "I thought the problem was volume. The real problem was vision."

Example (Brand): "We don't design to follow trends, we design to outlast them."

SATURDAY: COMMUNITY & CONVERSATION

Shift from broadcasting to bonding. Ask questions, create polls, or spotlight followers. This strengthens your tribe and keeps your audience warm.

Example: "What's one thing you'd never compromise on in your brand?"

Boss Law #112: A strong community beats a large audience, every time.

SUNDAY: REFLECT & RESET

Close the week with intention. Show gratitude, share a quote, or preview what's next.

Reflection = Retention.

It reminds your audience why they follow you, and why you're different. Example (Coach): "You don't need 1,000 ideas—you need one executed 1,000 times."

<u>IDEA</u> → <u>CREATE</u> → <u>POST</u> → <u>ENGAGE</u> → <u>REPURPOSE</u> → <u>REFLECT</u>

Each week is not a reset; it's a repetition of mastery. Your message compounds and your presence becomes permanent.

THE BOSS EXECUTION COMMAND CENTER

This is your weekly checklist for magnetic content execution.

Print it. Stick it above your desk. Use it like a ritual.

✔	TASK	GOAL
•	Batch create 3-5 posts on Sunday	Start the week prepared
•	Schedule Monday's and Tuesday's posts	Stay consistent early
•	Reply to all DMs daily	Build personal connections
•	Track engagement metrics weekly	Double down on what works
•	Review one old post for repurposing	Leverage your best hits
•	Reflect on progress Sunday night	Refine. Recalibrate. Repeat.

Boss Law #113: You don't need more ideas, you need more execution.

REFLECTION

When your content becomes consistent, your brand becomes predictable, and predictable value is the foundation of trust. Now that you've mastered the weekly content rhythm, it's time to build your Marketing Identity—your archetype. Because when your message matches your energy, your influence becomes inevitable.

THE BOSS MARKETING ARCHETYPES

"Your energy is your message."

Boss Law #114: People don't follow the best strategy; they follow the most aligned energy.

ENERGY OVER EFFORT

You can copy a caption. You can mimic a strategy. But you can't fake energy. Every brand that breaks through the noise shares one thing: Alignment.

When your marketing reflects who you truly are, not who you're pretending to be—it resonates like a frequency people can't ignore. Most people burn out not because they're lazy, but because they're misaligned. They're acting out of character, posting like someone else, chasing trends that don't fit their energy.

Bosses don't chase alignment. They build from it. Your archetype is the engine behind your marketing. It's not just how you show up, it's why people trust you when you do.

<u>The Mentor → The Maverick → The Motivator → The Scientist → The Storyteller → The Strategist → The Visionary</u>

Each one leads with a unique force. From logic to emotion, structure to inspiration, and all are powerful when mastered.

THE 7 ARCHETYPES

1. THE MENTOR: THE TRUSTED TEACHER

Energy: Calm Authority

Strengths: Clarity, Trust, Patience

Risks: Over-explaining, under-selling

Best For: Educators, coaches, consultants

The Mentor leads with wisdom, not hype. Their power is simplicity, turning complex ideas into clear steps that build immediate trust. They don't chase attention; they earn it through consistency and calm confidence.

Example (Coaching): "3 lessons I teach every new client before they earn $1."

Example (Product Brand): "How we engineered the perfect fabric after testing 37 samples."

**Boss Law #115: Authority isn't loud,
it's consistent clarity.**

2. THE MAVERICK: THE REBELLIOUS INNOVATOR

Energy: Bold and Disruptive

Strengths: Originality, Courage, Shock Value

Risks: Polarisation, Inconsistency

Best For: Challengers, Creators, Visionary Brands

The Maverick thrives on breaking rules and rewriting norms. They challenge conventions and make people rethink everything. Their audience doesn't want safety; they want shock that sparks thought.

Example (Coaching): "Why 99% of marketing advice is killing your brand."

Example (Product Brand): "We banned discounts—and sold out in 72 hours."

Boss Law #116: Rebellion with purpose
creates movement.

3. THE MOTIVATOR: THE FIRESTARTER

Energy: Passionate and Emotional

Strengths: Inspiration, Connection, Momentum

Risks: Over-hype, burnout if not backed by structure

Best For: Fitness, coaching, personal development

The Motivator leads with raw fire. Their energy makes people believe in themselves again. Every post feels like a rally cry, but the true power lies in directing that fire into practical transformation.

Example (Coaching): "You're one decision away from your first client."

Example (Product Brand): "Every hoodie we sell funds a youth sports program—wear purpose."

Boss Law #117: Inspiration without
direction is noise; inspiration with
structure is leadership.

4. THE SCIENTIST: THE DATA-DRIVEN ARCHITECT

Energy: Logical and Precise

Strengths: Systems, Credibility, Proof

Risks: Over-analysis, emotion disconnect

Best For: Agencies, tech, finance, optimisation

The Scientist's strength is certainty. They build trust through evidence and frameworks that eliminate guesswork. They teach through structure, giving the audience control over chaos.

Example (Coaching): "The 3 data points that predict a 5-figure month."

Example (Product Brand): "We tested 17 zippers, and only 1 passed our strength test."

**Boss Law #118: Proof is
the language of trust.**

5. THE STORYTELLER: THE EMOTIONAL CONNECTOR

Energy: Relatable and Human

Strengths: Empathy, Authenticity, Trust

Risks: Oversharing, lack of a clear offer

Best For: Lifestyle brands, personal brands, creators

The Storyteller wins hearts before wallets. Their strength is relatability, showing the scars behind the success. They remind the audience that growth is human.

Example (Coaching): "The first time I felt like a fraud, and what I did next."

Example (Product Brand): "We started with $300 and a garage printer. Now our tees ship worldwide."

**Boss Law #119: Vulnerability
creates visibility.**

6. THE STRATEGIST: THE MASTER PLANNER

Energy: Structured and Calm Leadership

Strengths: Frameworks, Predictability, Scaling

Risks: Over-engineering, slow action

Best For: Consultants, agencies, operations-driven brands

The Strategist doesn't talk about success; they map it. Their value lies in simplifying chaos into clear, scalable systems.

Example (Coaching): "The 3-phase offer system that closes clients weekly."

Example (Product Brand): "Our production line runs on a 3-step efficiency protocol that cuts costs by 42 %."

Boss Law #120: Systems set you free.

7. THE VISIONARY: THE LEGACY BUILDER

Energy: Futuristic and Purpose-Driven

Strengths: Big picture, influence, legacy

Risks: Disconnection from execution

Best For: Founders, movements, thought leaders

The Visionary leads through possibility. They see what doesn't exist yet and make people believe it can. They sell movement, not merchandise.

Example (Coaching): "I'm not teaching business—I'm teaching freedom."

Example (Product Brand): "We don't sell clothes; we sell belief in a generation that creates."

Boss Law #121: Vision without execution is an illusion. Execution without vision is labor.

IDENTIFYING YOUR ARCHETYPE

Take a moment and reflect:

1. What energises you most—teaching, challenging, inspiring, proving, relating, organising, or dreaming?
2. What type of content feels natural (not forced)?
3. How does your audience describe you when you're at your best?
4. Which Boss Law hits your gut the hardest?
5. What's your natural communication mode—emotion or logic?

Visualise the Archetype Compass

Axis	Description
Emotional ↔ Logical	Do you lead with story or strategy?
Reserved ↔ Bold	Do you attract through calm authority or dynamic energy?

Find your quadrant, that's your power zone.

ARCHETYPE INTEGRATION

Once you know your archetype:
- Build content that amplifies your natural energy.
- Design offers that mirror your style.
- Hire team members who balance your weaknesses.
- Repeat your message in the language your archetype speaks best.

Brand Voice Alignment Grid

Archetype	Tone	Visual Style	Core Content Format
Mentor	Educational and Clear	Clean layouts/ diagrams	Carousels / Guides
Maverick	Bold and Provocative	Contrast + Statement visuals	Reels / Short rants
Motivator	Passionate and Warm	Dynamic photos, motion	Inspirational videos
Scientist	Precise and Structured	Charts, infographics	Case studies
Storyteller	Relatable and Warm	Lifestyle shots/ textures	Story post
Strategist	Calm and Refined	Minimal professional	Framework slides
Visionary	Inspirational and Bold	Futuristic contrast	Keynote-style content

THE BOSS ARCHETYPE CODE

Boss Law #122: Authenticity is the ultimate strategy.

- Market from your energy, not from imitation.
- Build trust through alignment, not perfection.
- The more you act like you, the less competition you have.

When you discover and embody your true archetype, your marketing stops feeling like work and becomes a calling.

THE ORGANIC DOMINATION STRATEGY (THE BOSS 3C SYSTEM)

Boss Law #123: You don't need more followers. You need more follow-through.

THE POWER OF ORGANIC DOMINANCE

Paid ads can buy attention. But only organic authority earns loyalty. When you dominate organically, you don't chase customers—they find you, trust you, and refer you—The Boss 3C System. Create, Capture, Convert. Is the blueprint for turning your daily content and conversations into consistent clients without ever needing to "sell."

This is where consistency meets connection, and connection becomes conversion.

CREATE: BUILDING A CONTENT MACHINE THAT SELLS SILENTLY

Boss Law #124: Consistency compounds faster than virality.

Content isn't about shouting. It's about shaping perception. Your goal isn't to post—it's to position The Boss Content Compass. Every post should serve one of these purposes:

1. Awareness: Let them discover you.
2. Authority: Let them trust you.
3. Action: Let them take the next step.

Rotate content across these three pillars weekly. That keeps your brand dynamic and your audience engaged.

The 5 Daily Non-Negotiables:

1. Publish one piece of valuable content (post, story, or short).
2. Engage with 10 ideal clients' posts.
3. Start three genuine conversations.
4. Share one piece of personal insight (builds connection).
5. Track results and refine tomorrow.

This isn't a random activity. It's intentional momentum. The more predictable your output, the more predictable your income.

The Content Factory:

Inputs → Ideas, research, personal lessons.

Process → Frameworks, storytelling, editing.

Output → Posts that attract, teach, and inspire.

CAPTURE: TURNING ATTENTION INTO ACTION

Boss Law #125: Leads aren't found, they're forged through value.

Visibility without capture is vanity. Every impression should become a potential relationship.

The Capture Formula:

Give value → Offer clarity → Open conversation → Build trust

Here's how Bosses do it:

1. Lead Magnets That Convert
   - Quick, specific, result-driven (e.g., "3-Step Sales DM Framework").
   - One clear promise → one quick win.

2. The Magnetic Bio Test
   - Does your bio answer: Who you help, what you do, and what they get?
   - Example: "I help footballers take their game to the next level using designed drills proven to make them stand out"

3. DM Flow That Feels Human
   - Start with curiosity, not pitch.
   - Example: "Hey [Name], noticed you've been diving into our posts on [topic] How's that going for you right now?"
   - Listen before leading.
   - Transition naturally with: "Sounds like [problem] is slowing you down—I've got something that helps with that, want me to send it?"

This flow keeps you conversational, not confrontational. You're not pushing a sale, you're diagnosing a problem.

Awareness → Engagement → Question → Value Offer → Decision

CONVERT: FROM VALUE TO DECISION

Boss Law #126: Selling isn't convincing, it's aligning beliefs.

Conversion is not manipulation; it's clarity with confidence. People don't buy because you want them to. They buy because you show them the path they already believe in.

The Boss conversion process: S.O.L.D.
- Story: Frame the problem. "Here's what most people struggle with…"
- Offer: Present your solution clearly. "Here's how I help."
- Logic: Break down the how/why. "We use this system because it's proven to work."
- Decision: Invite action confidently. "Ready to get this fixed this week?"

When done right, the process feels natural. Like a next step, not a hard sell.

Handling Objections – Boss Style
- Money: "If you had this solved, what would it be worth to you?"
- Time: "If not now, when?"
- Doubt: "Let's focus on one win first—results create belief."

Remember, objections aren't rejection; they're requests for clarity.

THE DAILY DOMINATION CHECKLIST

Boss Law #127: Outcomes are built by decisions enforced daily.

Your empire grows one disciplined day at a time. Here's the system used by top Bosses for measurable progress:

Morning Reset (10 Minutes)
- Review yesterday's content performance.
- Pick one key story or lesson to share today.
- Write one line that sells belief, not product.

Day Actions (60 Minutes Total)
- Create and post (30 mins)
- Engage and start three convos (15 mins)
- Follow up with yesterday's prospects (15 mins)

Evening Debrief (5 Minutes)
- Log leads → Track conversions → Note what resonated

Weekly Reflection Prompts:
- What content created the most DMs?
- Who responded but didn't buy, and why?
- What belief did my audience need reinforced this week?

Visual Summary Table:

Stage	Goal	Tool	Outcome
Create	Attract	5 non-negotiables	Consistent visibility
Capture	Engage	DM flow/lead magnet	Qualified leads
Convert	Close	S.O.L.D. Framework	Paying clients

Organic dominance isn't about being everywhere. It's about being impossible to ignore where it matters. Show up with value, connect with conviction, and convert with integrity. That's the 3C difference, and that's how you become a Boss in motion.

PAID ADS SIMPLIFIED

Boss Law #128: Paid ads don't build momentum; they amplify it.

THE BOSS RULE OF ADS

Ads aren't the beginning, they're the multiplier. If your offer, message, and brand already create organic sales, paid ads turn that fire into an inferno.

Most people waste money because they advertise a broken message. Bosses test their message in the streets first (organic), then fuel it with paid reach.

Start ads only when you can answer three truths with confidence:
1. You've sold your offer at least once organically.
2. You know exactly who your buyer is and where they hang out.
3. You can communicate your value in one clear sentence.

When those align, ads become a precision weapon, not a slot machine.

WHERE TO RUN ADS (AND WHY)

Different platforms serve different stages of the buyer journey. Pick one battlefield, master it, and dominate before expanding.

1. Meta (Facebook + Instagram)

Best for: Coaches, consultants, e-commerce, and personal brands.

Use for:
- Lead generation (free guides, webinars, challenges).
- Retargeting followers and website visitors.
- Starting DM conversations with warm leads.

Real-World Example:

A fitness coach runs a $15/day local campaign: "Tired of training hard and seeing zero results? Join our 5-day reset plan—120 locals already in!"

Within one week, they book eight consultations and convert three into clients.

Pro Tip: Reels and Story ads feel native, use casual videos over studio shots.

2. TikTok Ads

Best for: Lifestyle products, courses, and brands targeting 18–35.

Use for:
- Quick, emotion-driven visibility.
- Short product demonstrations and user-generated clips.
- Retargeting profile visitors or video engagers.

Example, Streetwear Drop:

A brand films a 15-second clip of friends wearing their hoodie on a city rooftop.

Text Overlay: "Limited Drop. No Hype. Just Style."

Result: 1.8 M views in 4 days and inventory sold out in 72 hours.

Pro Tip: Keep videos under 20 seconds. Authenticity outperforms perfection.

3. YouTube Ads

Best for: Authority brands, mentorships, training programs.

Use for:
- Mini tutorials ending with a clear CTA.
- Story-driven ads ("how I did it" narratives).
- Retargeting website visitors or channel subscribers.

Example: An online academy runs a 2-minute video ad that explains its "Zero to First Client in 5 Days" method. The ad directs viewers to a free training page that generates 50 new leads per week.

Pro Tip: Hook viewers in the first 5 seconds. Every word after should earn the next.

4. Google Search & Display

Best for: High-intent services and local businesses.

Use for:
- Capturing active buyers ("near me," "best service").
- Retargeting display banners to stay visible.

Example: A branding agency runs Google Search ads for "logo design Sydney." They get qualified leads at $8 each and close projects worth $500+.

Pro Tip: Start with exact keywords, then expand to broader terms once profitable.

HOW TO STRUCTURE YOUR AD

Boss Law #129: Great ads don't sell;
they start conversations.

The Pain → Shift → Promise Formula

1. Pain: Call out the problem.
   "Still posting daily with no sales?"

2. Shift: Challenge beliefs.
   "It's not your product—it's your positioning."

3. Promise: Offer a result.
   "Fix your message and get clients in days."

Keep it short, mobile-first, and emotionally charged.

The Simple Ad Funnel

Ad → Free Value (guide/video) → Follow-Up → Offer
- 1 clear goal per funnel.
- 1 offer per campaign.
- 1 next step per page.

**Boss Law #130: Simplicity sells.
Complexity kills.**

HOW TO START SMALL
- Budget: $10–20/day per platform.
- Test 3 hooks × 3 creatives × 3 audiences.
- Kill low performers in 72 hours.
- Scale winners 20–30 % every 3 days.

Boss Tip: Don't raise budget too fast—stability beats speed.

THE AD CYCLE TRACKER

Day	Task	Goal
Monday	Launch/test 3 creatives	Find the strongest hook
Wednesday	Review metrics	Kill weak ads, scale winners
Friday	Check comments + engagement	Spot new angles
Sunday	Reinvest profits	Increase budget + expand reach

**Boss Law #131: Ads are athletes. They improve only
when you track their performance.**

METRICS THAT MATTER

Metric	Goal	If Low → Fix
Click Through Rate	1-3%	Improve visual + headline
Cost Per Lead	<$10	Tighten the lead offer
Return on Ad Spent	>2x	Adjust audience or ad angle

Boss Law #132: Don't chase vanity,
track velocity.

THE BOSS AD CHECKLIST

- Clear 1-sentence offer
- Strong "Pain → Shift → Promise" hook
- Video < 20 seconds OR Strong Post
- Headline answers "What's in it for me?"
- Direct call-to-action
- One goal per ad (funnel clarity)

Paid ads aren't magic; they're magnifiers. They take what's real and make it visible to the world. Master organic first. Build trust that converts. Then use ads to multiply the momentum you already earned.

Boss Law #133: The real ROI is not return
on ad spend, it's return on alignment.

THE AUTHORITY ENGINE

Boss Law #134: Consistency creates
credibility. Credibility creates authority.
Authority prints money.

AUTHORITY IS NOT THE SAME AS VISIBILITY

Most people chase visibility. Bosses build authority. Visibility just means people see you. Authority means people believe you. Follow you. Buy from you. Refer you. Quote you when you're not in the room.

Influence without proof is noise. Visibility without conviction is vanity. Followers without authority is a funeral for momentum.

Look at the brands that dominate categories:
- Apple doesn't need to trend. They dictate the standard.
- Nike doesn't convince, They command emotional loyalty.
- Rolex doesn't advertise discounts. Its name is the proof.
- Amazon doesn't explain. They've earned blind trust through consistency.

Authority is the competitive moat.

Once you have it, you stop fighting, and others start reacting. People do not buy what they see; they buy what they trust.

WHY AUTHORITY BEATS EXPOSURE

Anyone can go viral. Almost no one can stay relevant. Virality is a lottery. Authority is insurance. Virality is a moment. Authority is a monopoly. Exposure requires energy every time. Authority compounds, it does the work for you.

That is why amateurs chase eyes, and professionals build ecosystems.

When people perceive you as the one who knows, you don't have to lower price, beg for engagement, or justify your existence—your category bends around you.

Boss Law #135: The market bends around the one who is perceived as inevitable.

THE LONG-GAME VISIBILITY STRATEGY

Authority is not built by one tactic. It is built by repetition of identity.

There are three levers of long-game visibility:

1. Repetition of Message. Same philosophy, delivered in evolving forms.
2. Repetition of Results. Proof shown consistently over time.
3. Repetition of Presence. You show up whether you feel like it or not.

People need to see you enough times to trust that you're not a seasonal participant, but a permanent fixture in the category.

Most creators quit at 90 days. Authority begins at 365+. Think of the most respected people in any field; you didn't trust them after one video or one launch. You trusted them after years of consistency under pressure.

Boss Law #136: Longevity is the ultimate persuasion tactic.

THE AUTHORITY FLYWHEEL

Authority is not added manually; it is engineered to run continuously. The Authority Flywheel has four repeating phases:

<u>EDUCATE</u> → <u>DOCUMENT</u> → <u>REPURPOSE</u> → <u>RESURFACE</u> → <u>(repeat)</u>

1. Educate

You teach the market something they didn't fully understand before. You shift beliefs, frame thinking, or expose blind spots.

Education earns respect, and respect becomes leverage.

2. Document

You show the reality behind the expertise—work in motion, not just polished outcomes.

People trust what they can witness in progress. Documentation is how Tesla built anticipation before delivering products. Narrative before delivery.

3. Repurpose

You don't reinvent. You re-weaponise.

A post becomes a reel, a reel becomes a carousel, a carousel becomes an email, and an email becomes a keynote slide. Repetition is not redundancy; repetition cements identity.

4. Resurface

You bring back your greatest hits, your strongest ideas should not be posted once and buried. Every new follower needs to see your core beliefs again.

The brands with the strongest identities—Nike, Apple, Ferrari—repeat the same message for decades without apology.

> Boss Law #137: A message only becomes "old" to the creator, never to the market.

THE PURPOSE

This flywheel does two things simultaneously:

1. It removes friction for you, because you are not reinventing daily.
2. It builds familiarity for them because you are predictable in identity.

Authority is simply the compounding effect of controlled repetition over time.

Once the market knows what you stand for, who you serve, and what you refuse to compromise, you stop marketing to be seen and start marketing to be remembered.

AUTHORITY IN PRACTICE: WHERE IT SHOWS UP

Authority is not built in one channel; it reveals itself everywhere at once when done right. You know someone has authority when:

- Their name is mentioned in rooms they are not in.
- Their frameworks are repeated by people who never bought from them.
- Their competitors quote them indirectly.
- Their audience defends them without being asked.

> Boss Law #138: When you own the narrative, you don't compete. You set terms.

THE PARADOX OF EFFORT

The more authority you build, the less energy you need to maintain influence. In the beginning, effort is heavy:
- You show up daily.
- You publish without applause.
- You communicate consistently to cold eyes.

Authority has a delay curve; you work now for rewards that surface later. Then the curve flips. Once the authority is activated:

- Your name becomes a shortcut for trust.
- Buyers skip comparison and go straight to you.
- People assume quality without inspection.
- Opportunities arrive instead of being chased.

Authority turns output into gravity.

You stop reaching. Attention moves towards you.

THE MINDSET SHIFT REQUIRED FOR AUTHORITY

You cannot build authority if you think like a short-term performer. Influence at the highest level demands three internal conversions:

1. From noise to narrative.
   You stop posting for activity and start posting for positioning.

2. From trends to timelessness.
   You don't chase novelty, you build doctrine.

3. From ego to responsibility.
   Once people follow you, you stop creating for you. You create because leaders don't have the luxury of silence. Authority is a burden before it becomes a benefit.

THE INTERNAL RULES OF AN AUTHORITY-DRIVEN BRAND

These are non-negotiables that separate trusted names from forgettable content machines:

- You say less, but you say it better.
- You repeat core beliefs without apology.
- You display proof until doubt is impossible.
- You maintain standards when others relax.
- You let the results be louder than tone.
- You build for permanence, not applause.

Authority is not charisma. It is not volume. It is not personality luck. Authority is the byproduct of three things done relentlessly over time:

Conviction. Consistency. Competence delivered in public.

THE AUTHORITY ASSET STACK

Authority is not built by volume; it is built by owning the right assets that persist when you are not online. Here are the five assets that compound authority on autopilot:

1. Newsletter (Owned Audience)

Social platforms rent you attention. Email gives you ownership.

A weekly email, even 1 per week establishes:
- Permanence
- Thought leadership
- Memory of your message

Even Apple, Amazon, and Nike email because it is the only channel untouched by algorithm control.

> **Boss Law #139: If you don't own the audience, you don't own the leverage.**

2. Podcast Guesting (Borrowed Credibility)

You don't need your own podcast to gain authority; you tap into other people's distribution. Being interviewed positions you as:

- Validated by a third party
- Worthy of long-form attention
- Referenced beyond your own audience

A podcast appearance is a reputation multiplier, not just content.

3. Strategic Collaborations

You rise faster when you attach yourself to respected names. Not followers—perceived authorities. Micro-collabs work:

- Co-hosted live session
- Joint offer or challenge
- Shared newsletter segment
- Cross-promo between aligned audiences

Nike collaborates with Ronaldo → immediate category dominance.

Authority travels through association.

4. PR & Thought Placement

You don't need Forbes or CNN to win; those are legacy symbols. Modern PR = placed where your audience already consumes trust:

- Niche blogs
- Industry newsletters
- Creator YouTube breakdowns
- LinkedIn features
- Guest essays

You do not chase media to be seen. You leverage media to be positioned.

5. Signature Frameworks

Apple has "Think Different."
Nike has "Just Do It."
Amazon has "1-Click."

A single, repeatable idea defines authority brands. Readers, clients, and markets remember frameworks—not loose thoughts.

**Boss Law #140: You are not remembered
for effort, you are remembered for
the architecture of ideas.**

THE AUTHORITY AUTOMATION BLUEPRINT

Authority is not built by effort forever; it is sustained by systemisation. Here is how to run authority on autopilot in 2–3 hours per week:

Delegate / Automate:
- Repurposing past content → VA or automation tools
- Scheduling newsletters + posts → queued monthly
- Podcast outreach → one pre-written pitch scripted once
- PR submissions → quarterly batch system

You manually do only the thinking and the original voice. Everything else is engineered to repeat.

Boss Law #141: A Boss doesn't scale output.
A Boss scales systems that produce output.

METRICS THAT MATTER (THE AUTHORITY SCORECARD)

Your goal is not to "go viral."

Your goal is to become unavoidable.

Metric	Meaning	Signal
Mentions	You are referenced without a prompt	Recognition taking root
Reposts / Saves	Your thinking is becoming doctrine	Emerging influence
High-intent DMs	People approach you first	Trust threshold crossed
Referrals	Others sell you for free	Authority achieved

Boss Law #142: Authority is measured
in who talks about you when you
are silent.

THE DOCTRINE OF INEVITABILITY

Authority is not a tactic. It is not a hack. It is not a marketing stunt. Authority is the reward given to the person who out-thinks, out-shows, and out-stays everyone else. You do not become the Boss by force. You become the Boss by inevitability. When your message is repeated, when your name precedes you, when your presence equals trust—the market obeys without resistance.

Boss Law #143: You don't chase the throne, you build a presence so undeniable that the throne comes to you.

THE MARKETING BOSS TOOLKIT & FURTHER METRICS

Boss Law #144: Tools don't make you powerful; the disciplined use of them does.

Information creates understanding. Tools create results. That is the difference between readers and executors, between people who consume and people who collect cash.

You are not building a cute brand. You are engineering a machine. One that produces attention, authority, leads, demand, and revenue on command.

The amateur asks: "What do I post?"
The Boss asks: "What am I measuring and executing against?"
The amateur works from memory and motivation.
The Boss works from dashboards, templates, and repeatable systems.

This section is not theory. It is the operating system behind everything built in the previous sections, the infrastructure that prevents collapse and guarantees forward motion.

WHY THIS TOOLKIT EXISTS

Most people fail not because they lack effort but because they lack structure around that effort. People do not drift into success; they schedule it, track it, and enforce it.

This toolkit eliminates:

- Guessing
- Emotional decision making
- Inconsistent execution
- Forgetting your plan
- "Start again Monday" cycles

And replaces it with:

- Precision
- Proof
- Control
- Predictability
- Psychological advantage

> Boss Law #145: A system is a weapon;
> once installed, it removes weakness
> and uncertainty.

WHAT THIS SECTION WILL GIVE YOU

By the time you finish this section, you will have:

- A measurement framework so you know exactly what is working.
- A lead, content, and sales tracker to eliminate lost momentum.
- Printable templates ready to execute daily without thinking.
- Scripts and swipes you can use immediately without rewriting.
- A final summary sheet—1 page that directs your entire week.

This is the difference between:
- Hoping vs Projecting
- Effort vs Outcome
- Movement vs Progress
- Playing vs Winning

Systems turn ambition into something the world can't ignore.

HOW TO USE THIS TOOLKIT

Do not skim this section. Do not "understand it", install it.

For each tool:
1. Read the short instruction
2. Apply it immediately
3. Print or save it visibly
4. Execute it daily without negotiation

> Boss Law #146: If your systems are weak,
> your results are temporary.

THE METRICS THAT MATTER
(THE BOSS MEASUREMENT FRAMEWORK)

> Boss Law #147: What you don't measure,
> you forfeit control over.

Most people track the wrong things—followers, likes, impressions, noise. Bosses track only the numbers that predict and produce money. There are four categories of metrics that define the health of a marketing machine:

1. VISIBILITY METRICS: "Are people seeing me?"

These tell you if the market is aware of your existence:

- Reach/Impressions. How many eyes are entering your world.
- Profile visits. How many became curious enough to explore.
- New followers/subscribers. How many chose to stay.

If these are flat or declining, you do not have a discovery problem; you have a content and positioning problem.

2. ENGAGEMENT METRICS: "Are they paying attention?"

Visibility without engagement is ignored noise.

Track:
- Saves. "This is valuable."
- Shares. "This is worth spreading."
- Comments / Replies. "This changed how I think."

Likes mean nothing. Saves and shares mean impact.

> **Boss Law #148: Engagement is not vanity, it is evidence of relevance.**

3. CONVERSION METRICS: "Is attention becoming revenue?"

This is where amateurs look away and Bosses stare directly:

- Lead volume per week (inbound DMs, emails, opt-ins)
- Booked calls or cart-checkouts
- Closing rate (leads $\rightarrow$ buyers)
- Revenue per lead

If visibility is high and conversion is low $\rightarrow$ your offer or messaging is broken.

If conversion is high and visibility is low → your exposure is the bottleneck.

This is how a Boss diagnoses, not guesses.

4. AUTHORITY METRICS: "Am I becoming the default name?"

Authority is the highest metric—the one that most never reach.

Track:
- Unprompted mentions ("Someone referred me to you")
- Referrals without asking
- People quoting your frameworks
- Invitations to collaborate / guest / speak
- Clients closing without objection

Those signals mean the market is now working in your favor.

Boss Law #149: Authority is when the market sells you without your voice present.

THE BOSS MEASUREMENT TABLE

Use this every week—not monthly, not "when you feel like it."

Metric Class	Key Signals	If Weak - Fix
Visibility	Reach, profile visits, new audience	Improve hooks, positioning, and distribution
Engagement	Saves, shares, replies	Raise relevance, emotion, storytelling
Conversion	Leads, calls, sales, close rate	Refine offer, CTA, and lead qualification
Authority	Referrals, mentions, invites	Strengthen proof, consistency, and brand identity

This one table replaces months of confusion.

THE 7-DAY AUDIT RITUAL

Every Sunday, answer these seven questions:

1. Where did attention grow this week?
2. What content created the strongest reaction?
3. Which DM or lead source produced buyers?
4. What slowed or stalled momentum?
5. What needs to be doubled down on?
6. What needs to be eliminated immediately?
7. What will be executed first on Monday?

Do not build a brand on hope; make it on intelligence.

> Boss Law #150: Intelligence is not knowing.
> It is measuring and adjusting without ego.

THE FULL MARKETING BOSS TOOLKIT (TEMPLATES, SCRIPTS & TRACKERS)

> Boss Law #151: A Boss doesn't wait for clarity;
> a Boss installs clarity.

This section gives you the done-for-you execution tools so nothing is left to guesswork. Each tool below follows the hybrid format: Short instruction → Immediate template you can use.

TOOL 1: THE WEEKLY LEAD & SALES TRACKER

Purpose: So no conversation, lead, or sale slips through cracks again.

Use it: Update once daily, takes 3 minutes.

Template:

Name	Source	Status (Cold/Warm/Hot)	Last Touch	Next Action	Value
Alex G	IG DM	Warm	Feb 7	Send case study	$500 pkg
–	–	–	–	–	–

Instruction: If a name has no "Next Action," it is a dead lead. Every lead must live in motion.

TOOL 2: THE DM CONVERSION SCRIPT (NO SPAM, NO BEGGING)

Purpose: Convert conversations without sounding desperate.

Template:

Step 1. Open without selling: "Noticed you've been checking out the [topic] posts—what are you working on right now?"

Step 2. Diagnose the problem: "What's the biggest thing slowing you down with that?"

Step 3. Permission-based transition: "I have something that fixes exactly that—want me to show you?"

Step 4. Close cleanly: "If you want, we can lock this in today and get you moving this week."

Boss Law #152: A close is just the moment
the right solution meets the right problem
with confidence.

TOOL 3: THE 10-MINUTE CONTENT DECISION FRAMEWORK

Never wonder what to post again. Before posting, answer these three:

1. Which Pillar? (Value / Story / Proof / CTA)
2. What is the single belief I want to change?
3. Does this move someone closer to buying? (Yes = Post. No = Delete.)

This removes emotional noise and replaces it with direction.

TOOL 4: THE CALLBACK OFFER SCRIPT (FOR WARM LEADS WHO WENT SILENT)

Use exactly as written:

"Still want help with this, or should I close your file for now?"

Silence turns into decisions. Low power language creates ghosts—clarity creates motion.

TOOL 5: THE WEEKLY CONTENT MAP (BOSS RHYTHM)

Day	Focus	Goal
Monday	Value / Education	Build Authority
Tuesday	Story	Build Connection
Wednesday	Proof	Build Trust
Thursday	CTA	Create Demand
Friday	Hybrid	Deepen Positioning
Saturday	Community	Start Conversations
Sunday	Reflection	Reset Strategy

Boss Law #153: Discipline beats motivation, schedule beats intention.

TOOL 6: THE REFERRAL SCRIPT

Send after successful delivery:

"Enjoyed working with you—do you know 1–2 people who would benefit from the same result?"

Clients recruit better than ads.

TOOL 7: THE "NO FAIL" WEEK START PROTOCOL

Every Monday morning:

1. Review leads
2. Send three "open loops"
3. Publish one high-authority post
4. Start five new conversations
5. Score the week before it starts

The week is won before noon Monday.

INTERNAL INSTALLATION RULE

None of these tools work if they stay in theory.

Print them.

Post them on your wall.

Use them until they become muscle memory.

THE MARKETING BOSS OPERATING COMMAND

This is the compressed battlefield sheet. The page you execute from, not think about. Tape it to your wall. Open it every morning before anything else.

I. WEEKLY TARGETS

Decide these BEFORE the week begins.

Leads to generate: _______________________________

Conversations to start: _______________________________

Sales to close: _______________________________

Revenue target: _______________________________

II. DAILY NON-NEGOTIABLES

If these are done, the business grows. If not, it doesn't.

- Publish one high-signal piece of content
- Start five new conversations
- Follow up with five dormant leads
- Show one piece of proof (result, win, progress, testimonial)
- Make one invitation to buy

III. LEAD STATUS MAP

Every person in your world is in one of three columns—never "unknown."

COLD	WARM	HOT
Aware but not speaking	In conversation	Ready to buy or deciding

Rule: No lead leaves the week without a next action.

IV. THE 4-PART MESSAGE CHECK

Before hitting "post" or "send," check:

- Is there emotion?
- Is there clarity?
- Is there relevance?
- Is there a path forward?

If any answer is NO → rewrite.
If all four are YES → publish.

V. THE SUNDAY RESET (7-QUESTION REVIEW)

1. What created the most response this week?
2. What created actual leads, not likes?
3. What stalled and must be cut?
4. What must be doubled?
5. What problems emerged?
6. What will be executed on Monday at 9am?
7. Who must hear from me tomorrow?

**Boss Law #156: A Boss does not start weeks blind.
A Boss begins weeks pre-decided.**

VI. THE 30-DAY AUTHORITY GAUGE

Each week, answer yes or no:

- Did someone mention you without you prompting?
- Did someone refer a client?
- Did someone quote or repost you?
- Did someone approach YOU to buy, not the other way around?
- Did you repeat your core message at least 5 times?

If fewer than 3 are YES, your authority engine is not yet firing—return to consistency.

VII. THE FINAL COMMAND

This page is not decoration. This is your marching order. It replaces hesitation with direction, emotion with execution, and randomness with design.

Boss Law #157: When systems exist, excuses die.

END OF THE MARKETING BOSS PLAYBOOK

You now hold the machinery that makes you visible, memorable, and in demand.

Not by chance. By engineered positioning, repeated authority, and systems that remove inconsistency.

Marketing is no longer something you "attempt." It is something you run—on purpose, on schedule, with leverage.

You have installed:
- A message people remember.
- A presence that compounds without you.
- A strategy that converts attention into demand.
- A toolkit that kills hesitation and replaces it with execution.

This is the point where amateurs slow down—Bosses do the opposite.

**Boss Law #158: Marketing creates the demand.
Sales capture the reward.**

The job of Marketing is complete when the market arrives warm. The job of Sales begins when the market is listening.

TRANSITION: ENTER THE BOSS SALES PLAYBOOK

What comes next is not "more tactics". It is the discipline of turning interest into income repeatedly, without emotional friction.

You are not learning how to talk to people. You are learning how to lead decisions.

You are not learning how to convince. You are learning how to remove resistance.

You are not learning how to pitch. You are learning how to close cleanly, confidently, and without apology.

The Marketing Playbook made you visible.

The Sales Playbook will make you paid.

THE BOSS SALES PLAYBOOK

THE PSYCHOLOGY OF DECISION

Sales is leadership, not persuasion.

Most people think sales is about talking someone into a decision. It isn't.

Sales is the transfer of certainty—from the person who has it to the person who lacks it. When a prospect is on the fence, two forces are battling inside them: Fear of loss vs Desire for change.

Sales is not about adding more desire. It's about neutralising the fear. People don't say NO because they don't want the result. They say NO because they don't trust:

- themselves
- the process
- the provider
- the timing
- the risk

Sales dies not in the wallet, but in uncertainty.

SALES IS A DECISION-LEADING PROCESS

Weak sales tries to convince. Boss sales guides a decision that was already forming inside them. You are not introducing a new idea—you are accelerating one they already had but did not act on.

Anyone who books a call, replies to a DM, or studies your content is already halfway in. If they were truly uninterested, they would be invisible.

Sales is not about pressure. It is about leadership:
- You lead the thinking
- You lead the framing of their problem
- You lead the urgency
- You lead the clarity
- You lead the close

> **Boss Law #160: If you do not lead the decision, the prospect will default to inaction, and inaction always wins by default.**

THE MENTAL MODEL OF A BUYER

Before someone buys, they run five subconscious checks:

Internal Question	Translation
"Do they get my problem?"	Empathy test
"Can they solve it?"	Competence test
"Will it work for me?"	Relevance test
"Is it worth the cost?"	Value test
"Is now the right time?"	Risk test

A closer doesn't wait for these thoughts; they answer them before they surface. That is why elite sales sounds calm, direct, inevitable—because it is engineered around the way humans actually decide.

WHY MOST PEOPLE FAIL AT SALES

They approach sales like a performer, not an authority.

They:
- Argue instead of diagnosing
- Chase instead of direct
- Talk instead of asking
- Pitch instead of clarity
- Wait for "readiness" instead of engineering commitment

And the root = emotional attachment.

People fail at sales when they need the sale. Neediness is the loudest form of weakness.

Boss Law #161: You cannot lead someone you are trying to impress.

THE CORE SHIFT: FROM ASKING TO QUALIFYING

An amateur asks for a "yes." A Boss decides whether this person earns access. A shift in tone changes everything.

From: "Are you interested in working together?"

To: "Before we go further, I need to make sure you're actually someone I can get results for."

This reframes the power dynamic entirely. The buyer is no longer evaluating you; you are considering them. People buy when they feel led, not when they feel chased.

Sales is not a performance. Sales is the moment leadership is tested in real time. If you are not certain, they cannot be certain. If you do not lead, they will retreat. If you hesitate, they will delay.

Sales is the art of making action feel safer than staying the same. In the next section, we transition from the psychology to the mechanics.

POSITIONING FOR THE CLOSE

Make "yes" the default, not the exception.

Boss Law #162: If you position correctly, the close is a formality, not a fight.

Most people try to sell at the end of a conversation. Bosses pre–close before the sale even begins. Sales don't start when you make an offer; sales start the moment they come into contact with your positioning.

If the positioning is correct, a sale is not a "persuasion event." It is the logical conclusion.

THE PRE-CLOSE POSITIONING TRIAD

Before a prospect ever hears a price, three beliefs must already be installed:

1. "This person understands my exact problem." (EMPATHY positioning. "They see me clearly.")

2. "This person has solved this before." (COMPETENCE positioning. "They are capable, not theoretical.")

3. "This person is the best option for me, not just an option." (PRE-EMINENCE positioning. "Why would I look elsewhere?")

If those beliefs are installed, price becomes a detail, not a barrier.

THE PRE-EMINENCE FRAMING SHIFT

You are not "an alternative." You are the only sane choice for someone serious about solving this problem. You do this by claiming territory:

Instead of: "I help people with fitness coaching."

You assert: "I work with people who are done trying random programs and ready for a serious, structured transformation with timelines and accountability."

One frames you as an option.
One frames you as a filter.

Boss Law #163: You do not compete when you disqualify the unserious.

HOW TO CREATE A DEFAULT YES USING FRAMES

Before you ever make an offer, you implant frames that make "yes" feel inevitable:

Frame 1. The Inevitability Frame: "You're clearly not someone who wants to stay stuck—you're already taking action by having this conversation."

Frame 2. The Consequence Frame: "If nothing changes this month, what does that cost you?"

Frame 3. The Future-Pace Frame: "If we do this right, 90 days from now this problem is permanently removed."

Frame 4. The Leadership Frame: "My job here isn't to convince you—it's to direct you to the correct next step."

These frames make the sale feel like alignment, not pressure.

THE POWER OF DISQUALIFICATION

Nothing increases desire like selective access.

Say lines like:

- "Before we continue, I need to make sure you're actually someone I can help."
- "I don't take on clients who aren't ready to execute immediately."
- "If we do this, you must be all-in."
- "Some people aren't ready for this level, and that's fine."

Disqualification does three things instantly:

1. Raises your perceived value.
2. Shifts the power dynamic in your favor.
3. Filters out the time-wasters before price ever comes up.

Boss Law #164: Scarcity is not a marketing tactic. It is a quality filter.

Price resistance happens when positioning is weak. Objections happen when the frame is weak. Chasing happens when authority is weak. Sales are not won during the close; sales are won in how you set the stage before the close. You are not trying to get agreement at the end. You are engineering an agreement all the way through.

THE CONVERSATION ARCHITECTURE

WHY CONTROLLED CONVERSATIONS CLOSE & "WINGING IT" FAILS

Boss Law #165: The mind that controls the structure controls the decision.

Sales is not a social exchange; it is a leadership exchange. When a prospect is not led, they default to fear, delay, and safety. Not because they don't want the result, but because no one controlled the path to it. People don't buy when they feel convinced. People buy when they feel led and safe.

CONTROL = COMFORT FOR THE BUYER

Most amateurs avoid control because they think it creates pressure.

In reality:
- Lack of control = anxiety
- Control = relief

Humans relax when someone responsible takes command: a pilot, a surgeon, a coach, a lawyer, and in this context, you.

Control is not force. Control is clarity.

Boss Law #166: People follow structure because structure feels safer than indecision.

THE SALE IS NOT AT THE END: IT HAPPENS THROUGHOUT

Amateurs "pitch" at the end. Bosses pre-close by how they run the entire conversation. A close is not a final move; it is the end of a controlled sequence.

WITHOUT STRUCTURE, YOU LOSE THE FRAME

When you do not lead, this happens:

- ✗ Prospect talks in circles
- ✗ You answer random questions
- ✗ Price becomes the focus instead of pain
- ✗ You chase, justify, and lose authority

With structure, the opposite happens:

- ✓ Prospect follows your direction
- ✓ Pain and urgency stay centered

- ✓ Price becomes a detail, not a barrier
- ✓ Decision feels logical, not risky

Boss Law #167: Sales is not persuasion;
it is engineered certainty applied in sequence.

PHASE 1: CONTROL & CALIBRATE

Objective: take leadership in the first 30–60 seconds.

Boss Law #168: The person who frames
first becomes the authority.

Control Openers (Choose One & Use as-is)

Authority Open: "Here's how we'll do this: I'll ask a few targeted questions to understand where you are, then I'll tell you what makes sense next. Sound good?"

Qualification Open: "Before I make any recommendations, I need to understand if you're actually someone I can help, so I'll lead with a few key questions."

Efficiency Open: "To keep this efficient, I'll ask first, you answer straight, and then we'll decide if moving forward makes sense. Deal?"

All three communicate the same message: "I am leading this, not you."

Tone & Delivery Rules for Phase 1

- Speak slower than you usually do (authority = unhurried)
- End sentences down, not up (certainty, not question energy)
- No laughter, no fillers, no apology language
- Minimal words—maximum clarity

What Not to Do in Phase 1

✘ Do not mirror their casual tone
✘ Do not let them open with their story first
✘ Do not start with price, process, or features
✘ Do not answer ANY questions yet, you lead first

Why this Phase Matters

If you don't establish control at the start, you will spend the rest of the call chasing it back.

Control claimed early = resistance drops later.

> Boss Law #169: If you do not lead the first minute, you will lose the last minute.

PHASE 2: DIAGNOSIS

Objective: Make the prospect confront the real cost of not solving the problem.

> Boss Law #170: A buyer does not move because you want the sale; they move because you made their current reality unacceptable.

You are not "getting to know them."

You are forcing clarity about the pain, cost, and consequences of staying the same.

The 6 Diagnosis Questions (Use exactly as written)

Ask in order. Do not soften them.

1. "What exactly is the problem you're trying to solve?". Not the story, the core issue.
2. "How long have you been dealing with this?". Time = proof of failure without help.
3. "What have you tried already, and why didn't it work?". Makes them admit DIY and cheap solutions failed.
4. "If nothing changes in the next 90 days, what happens?". This creates consequences.
5. "And if you do fix this properly, what becomes possible?". This creates hope and future pull.
6. "So is this something you want solved now, or later?". This forces a self-declared timeline.

Examples (3 Contexts)

COACHING / ACADEMY EXAMPLE
- "What's the gap in your player development right now?"
- "How long has it stalled?"
- "What did you try—private sessions, programs—why didn't they change it?"
- "If nothing changes before next season, what does that cost him?"
- "If he levels up now, what opens—trials, selection, scholarships?"
- "So is this a priority now, or later?"

SERVICE-BASED EXAMPLE (Designer / Agency)
- "What's broken in your current branding/marketing?"
- "How long have you tolerated it?"
- "What have you already paid for that didn't fix it?"
- "What does another 3 months of weak brand cost you?"
- "If we fix it, what does it unlock—credibility, higher pricing, new clients?"
- "So are we solving this now, or parking it again?"

PRODUCT EXAMPLE (e.g. Apparel / Equipment)

- "What's the issue with what you're using now?"
- "How long have you been settling for that?"
- "What cheaper options have you tried, and why did they fail?"
- "What do you lose if you keep using low-grade gear another season?"
- "If you upgrade, what changes—performance? confidence? perception?"
- "So is the upgrade a now move or a later move?"

Rules During Diagnosis

- YOU ask. They answer. You do not explain anything yet.
- Do not react emotionally; stay neutral and slow.
- Silence after key questions is a weapon; let them fill it.

> Boss Law #171: Urgency is not created by
> hype. It is extracted from the truth they
> already live in.

PHASE 3: FUTURE FRAME + FIT FILTER

Objective: Shift them from explaining the past to committing to the future and flip the power dynamic so they must qualify for YOU.

> Boss Law #172: People commit hardest to
> the futures they verbalise, and to
> the standards they must earn.

Step A. Future Frame (Make them state the upside out loud)

You now move them from pain → possibility.

Use 1–2 of these lines:

- "If this gets solved properly, what does life look like 90 days from now?"

- "What becomes possible for you once this is fixed?"
- "What's the win-state we're aiming at if you execute?"

Let them talk. What they say becomes ammunition later.

Step B. Fit Filter (You now evaluate THEM, not the other way around)

You are no longer trying to be chosen; you are seeing if they qualify.

Use one of these:
- "Before I even consider working with someone, I need to know they actually follow through. Are you that type?"
- "I don't take people who just 'want to try', I take people who execute. Where do you fall?"
- "If I show you the path and timeline, are you the kind of person who follows through without disappearing?"

This flips the hierarchy instantly.

You are not seeking approval. They are earning access.

Boss Law #173: The moment they try to impress you, the sale is 80% done.

Step C. Qualification Consequence

You make it clear there is a standard, not a slot.

Example lines:
- "If you're not ready, I'd rather you say it. I don't work with half-committed people."
- "If you want comfort, stay where you are. This is for people who want change."
- "Once we start, there is no drifting. you execute or you don't get in."

This is not aggression; it is identity shaping. People pay to step into standards higher than their current behavior.

Tone & Silence

This phase is not energetic. It is cold, slow, and surgical.

Key rule: Ask → stop talking → let their discomfort break before you speak again.

Silence = psychological leverage.

Once they confirm they are "someone who executes," you finish this phase with:

Lock-in line. "Good. Then if the solution makes sense, there is no reason we leave this call without a decision, agreed?"

If they say "yes", you just pre-closed before the offer.

> **Boss Law #174: The close begins the moment someone agrees that not deciding is no longer acceptable.**

PHASE 4: DECISION LEAD-IN

Objective: Secure commitment to decide before you reveal the solution or price.

> **Boss Law #175: Never present an offer to an undecided mind.**

The worst mistake amateurs make is pitching while the prospect is still mentally "half-in." We eliminate that by forcing a binary commitment first.

The Decision Agreement Questions (Pick 1–2)

These must be asked before presenting your offer:

- "Based on everything you told me, it sounds like this is not a 'later' problem—it's a now problem. Correct?"
- "If I show you a path that solves this properly, are you prepared to take action on it?"
- "You said staying the same is not an option—so you're making a decision today, yes?"

You do not continue until they say YES.

If they hesitate, do not pitch; re-diagnose the fear.

If they Hesitate here

Use one of these redirect lines:

- "Hesitation tells me you're not fully convinced this needs to be solved now. What part still feels safe to delay?"
- "I don't move forward with people who are unsure, help me understand what you're protecting by waiting."

You do not rescue them, you expose the fear. Once clarity returns, ask the decision line again.

Once they Agree to Decide

Now you anchor expectation before the offer:

- "Good. Then I'll lay out what solving this looks like, and at the end we decide—yes or no—not 'think about it.' Agreed?"
- "I don't do follow-up begging, we decide today based on facts. Fair?"

When they say "Agreed", two psychological shifts happen:

1. They have pre-committed to a decision—not escape.
2. You have removed "I'll think about it" before it arises.

Boss Law #176: The most powerful objection is the one you eliminate before it is spoken.

Red Flag Interpretation (What early signals mean)

If at this stage they say things like:

- "Well, it depends…"
- "I just want to hear pricing…"
- "I'll need to check with someone…"

These are not objections; they are signals of unresolved fear. You do not move to price. You loop back to diagnosis or consequence until certainty returns.

Transition to Offer

Once decision commitment is secured, you transition with a calm authority line:

- "Alright. Here is exactly what solving this looks like."

No hype.
No energy spike.
Just inevitability.

Failure Modes & Power Recovery

Objective: What to do the moment control is lost or the prospect derails the conversation.

Boss Law #177: The sale is not lost when they object, it is lost when you lose the frame.

Every derailment is one of only four categories:

1. They change the topic.
2. They ask premature questions.
3. They deflect with vagueness.
4. They retreat into delay language.

Below is how to regain control in each case.

1. When they change the topic.
Example: "Yeah, but what platform do you use?"/"What is the schedule like?"/"Is this Zoom or in-person?"

Recovery line: "I'll cover that if we decide it's a fit—right now I need to stay on the actual problem or this won't be productive."

2. When they ask about price too early.
Never answer price before pre-close.

Recovery line: "Price comes after we verify that solving this is a now-or-never move and that you actually want the result—otherwise any number is meaningless. Let's stay with the decision first."

Now continue your frame.

3. When they go vague.
Example: "I just need to think about everything."

Recovery line: "Think about what specifically—the solution, the timing, or the trust?"

Vagueness shattered.

4. When they retreat into delay.
Example: "I might do this later."/"Maybe after X settles down."

Recovery line: "What changes between now and later that suddenly makes you ready—or is that just a comfortable escape plan?"

Silence after this is intentional.

> **Boss Law #178: The job is not to remove discomfort, the job is to remove illusion.**

Do Not Ever Do These 3 Things

✗ Explain yourself to regain control
✗ Chase their approval or reassurance
✗ Answer tactical questions before commitment

Every time you justify, you drop in status.
Every time you chase, you make their fear stronger.
Every time you answer prematurely, you give control away.

Phrases that Immediately Reclaim Frame

Use these anytime energy slips:

- "Pause—we're off-topic. Come back."
- "That's not the decision on the table right now."
- "You're asking future questions to avoid the present one."
- "Let's be adults. Are you serious about solving this or not?"

> **Boss Law #179: Control recovered is more powerful than control never challenged.**

Tonality, Silence & Delivery Laws

Words don't close—delivery does. You are not just communicating information, you are transmitting certainty, control, inevitability.

> **Boss Law #180: The same sentence spoken with weak tonality loses. Spoken with authority, it closes.**

Tonality Laws

1. Speak slower than normal.
   Fast = nervous. Slow = in control.

2. End sentences down, not up.
   Upward inflection = asking for permission.
   Downward inflection = decisions are made here.

3. Cut filler language.
   No: "kind of… maybe… I think… just… honestly…"
   These are signals of insecurity.

4. Authority is calm, not loud.
   You do not sell with energy, you sell with composure.

> **Boss Law #181: The calm voice dominates the uncertain mind.**

The Weapon of Silence

Silence is not a pause; it is a pressure chamber. After critical lines (diagnosis, consequence, commitment), you STOP TALKING.

Silent seconds do the closing for you because:

- They are forced to confront their truth
- They reveal real objections instead of surface ones
- They feel the weight of indecision

Rule: After asking a decisive question, no sound until they answer. If you speak first, you surrender power.

Pace & Rhythm Rules

DO NOT:
- Talk at their pace
- Match their nervous energy
- Fill every gap
- Rush to the close

DO:
- Control tempo
- Use pauses like punctuation
- Keep sentences short and direct
- Let consequences land without rescue

Posture & Breathing (Even on calls/DM)

- Shoulders down → not tense
- Breathing through nose → calm authority
- Stillness → no fidgeting, no "performance energy"

Humans read subtext even without video. Your nervous system sells before your words do.

> **Boss Law #182: They don't buy the offer;
> they buy the nervous system delivering it.**

THE PERFECT CONVERSATION (FULL SCRIPT WITH ANNOTATIONS)

This is a complete example of a controlled sales conversation executed from start to decision. We will use a hybrid example (service/coaching context) so it applies broadly. Annotations in [brackets] explain why each line is used.

OPEN — CONTROL & CALIBRATE

YOU: "Here's how we'll run this—I'll ask a few targeted questions to understand where things stand, then I'll tell you what the right move is. Sound good?"

PROSPECT: "Yeah, that works."

[Frame established. You lead, they follow]

DIAGNOSIS — EXTRACT THE PROBLEM

YOU: "What exactly is the core problem you're trying to solve right now?"
PROSPECT: "I'm not getting clients even though I've been posting."

YOU: "How long has that been the case?"
PROSPECT: "Maybe 5 or 6 months."

YOU: "And what have you already tried that didn't fix it?"
PROSPECT: "I tried dropping prices and doing more content, but nothing changed."

[They admit DIY has failed. This increases openness to leadership]

YOU: "If nothing changes in the next 60–90 days, what does that cost you?"

PROSPECT (hesitates): "A lot. I can't afford another quarter like this."

SILENCE: you let the weight land.
(Silence forces emotional truth to surface)

FUTURE FRAME + FIT FILTER

YOU: "If this gets solved properly—if leads and sales become consistent—what becomes possible for you?"
PROSPECT: "I'd feel stable. I could stop stressing over bills."

YOU: "Before I even consider making a recommendation, I need to know—when you commit to something, do you actually execute or do you drift?"
PROSPECT: "No, if I commit—I go all in."

YOU: "Good. I don't take on people who want to 'try' only those ready to fix it now, not later."

[Qualification flips power, they try to earn your approval now]

DECISION PRE-FRAME

YOU: "So if I show you a path that fixes this properly, you're prepared to make a decision on it—not think about it for a week. Correct?"
PROSPECT: "Yes."

YOU: "Perfect. Then I'll lay out exactly what solving this looks like, and we decide at the end—yes or no. Not 'maybe'. Agreed?"
PROSPECT: "Agreed."

[Now the pitch can begin, the mind is positioned]

ANNOTATION SUMMARY

You did not:
- Justify yourself
- Pitch early
- Lose control
- Answer random questions
- Try to "be liked"

You did:
- Lead from the first sentence
- Make them confront pain and cost
- Make them verbalise desire
- Make them qualify for access
- Secure a decision commitment before presenting the offer

**Boss Law #183: By the time you pitch,
the close was already engineered.**

SUMMARY: WHAT YOU NOW CONTROL

You now have a repeatable structure that removes all randomness from sales conversations:

PHASE 1. CONTROL & CALIBRATE: (You set the frame, no equal footing)

PHASE 2. DIAGNOSIS: (You extract pain, cost, and failed attempts)

PHASE 3. FUTURE FRAME + FIT FILTER: (You shift to possibility and make them qualify)

PHASE 4. DECISION LEAD-IN: (You secure commitment to decide before presenting anything)

With these four phases, the prospect is no longer thinking, drifting, or evaluating you; they are following you. You do not "earn the sale at the close" you EARN IT THROUGH ARCHITECTURE.

> **Boss Law #184: A sale is not won at the end. It is prevented from being lost at the beginning.**

WHY THIS MATTERS BEFORE WE PRESENT THE OFFER

Amateurs present offers to undecided minds. Bosses present offers only once the decision state is pre-locked. That is the difference between:

- "I need to think about it"

  vs

- "This makes sense, let's do it."

The following section will show you how to present your offer without pitching, convincing, or performing—using a delivery style that sounds inevitable, not salesy.

PSYCHOLOGICAL INEVITABILITY

Where "yes" becomes the only intelligent conclusion.

Before the Close: You Don't Convince. You Corner.

> **Boss Law #185: A sale is not about making "yes" attractive. It is about making "no" indefensible.**

Most people try to make their offer sound good. A Boss makes not buying look like self-inflicted sabotage. Persuasion is not about adding benefits, it is about removing alternatives until reality has one exit.

THE 3 FORCES YOU CONTROL BEFORE THE PITCH

You create inevitability by engineering three psychological states:

1. Constraint — They believe there are no other viable paths.
2. Exposure — They confront the cost of not acting.
3. Compression — Time and consequence are not allowed to stretch.

Without these, a prospect can "afford" to hesitate. With these, hesitation feels stupid. Not neutral.

Force #1: Constraint (Erase the illusion of options)

You do not say your solution is "good." You make every other path look structurally doomed. Examples:

- "You've already tried the 'do nothing' path, it kept you stuck."
- "DIY has failed for months—repeating it is not neutral, it's regression."
- "A cheaper solution already proved it can't carry the weight."

You leave them nowhere "reasonable" to escape.

**Boss Law #186: Alternatives must die
before commitment is born.**

Force #2: Exposure (Make the cost of inaction conscious)

People don't fear payment; they fear confronting the truth. You force them to look at what "no" really costs—in math, not emotion.

- "Another quarter like this equals another $____ lost."
- "Staying here locks in the same life for another 6–12 months."
- "If your current approach were going to work, it would have by now."

You don't shame them, you expose the arithmetic.

Boss Law #187: When the cost of staying exceeds the cost of moving, the close is already done.

Force #3: Compression (Remove temporal escape routes)

"Later" is the most expensive lie people tell themselves. You collapse the illusion that time improves readiness:

- "Nothing arriving next month creates more readiness than today."
- "Delay doesn't reduce cost—it compounds it."
- "Later is a padded word for never."

You make delay feel like an active decision to lose.

Boss Law #188: You do not pressure decisions, you compress delusion.

THE RESULT

By the time you present the offer:

- "Yes" is not about you
- "Yes" is not about price
- "Yes" is not even about desire

"Yes" is the only option that keeps them aligned with reality and self-respect.

You did not sell.

You eliminated every exit but the correct one.

Boss Law #189: You don't push people into yes, you trap them out of no.

ENFORCEMENT FRAMES

Language that makes backing out psychologically expensive. Once you have constrained options, exposed cost, and compressed time, you must protect the frame so they cannot mentally retreat.

Boss Law #190: People don't back out because the offer is wrong. They back out because the exit was left open.

Enforcement frames are not "persuasion lines". They are cognitive traps that make retreat feel irrational or self-betraying.

Enforcement Frame #1: Reality > Preference

You don't argue with them, you pin them to the facts they already admitted:

"You're not deciding between this or something better. You already ruled out everything else. The only real fork is fix it now vs stay stuck."

The moment they hear their own logic thrown back at them, escape becomes a contradiction.

Enforcement Frame #2: Now Vs Never, Not Now Vs Later

You do not let them think "later" is neutral—you force the binary truth:

"This isn't now vs later. It's now vs not at all. Every later has produced the same outcome."

You're not debating motivation, you're exposing pattern repetition.

Enforcement Frame #3: Identity Trap

You tie the decision to who they claimed they are or want to be:

"Somebody who is actually done with this problem moves now. If you don't—you're not done with it, you're negotiating with it."

You don't shame. You mirror.

**Boss Law #191: Identity always settles
the argument faster than logic.**

Enforcement Frame #4: Cost of Retreat

You make going backwards feel more "expensive" than proceeding:

"If you walk back after admitting all of this, you're choosing the exact conditions you said you can't live with."

Not an opinion. A consequence.

Enforcement Frame #5: No-Escape Clarifier

This frame removes all fog and forces a naked decision:

"So we are left with two truths: You don't want to stay here, and the only alternative to staying here is this. Which truth do you align with now?"

There is no third path. You seal the walls before the close.

**Boss Law #192: The close happens when
the exit becomes psychologically expensive,
not when the offer becomes attractive.**

DECISION COMPRESSION

Collapsing hesitation without pressure or emotion.

**Boss Law #193: Hesitation is not
uncertainty; it is oxygen. Remove
the oxygen, and the hesitation dies.**

People do not stall because they need more information; they stall because they still believe time reduces consequences. Decision Compression removes that belief.

Compression Rule #1: Remove the illusion of a "better moment"

"If there was a smarter time than now, we would name it and wait for it—but we both know it doesn't exist."

This forces them to admit that delay is emotional, not strategic.

Compression Rule #2: Convert time into loss, not space

You collapse time by reframing it as an active cost:

"Every week this sits, you are compounding the exact conditions you're trying to escape."

Not neutral. Not harmless. Compounding.

Compression Rule #3: Shorten the horizon of responsibility

Humans freeze when decisions feel too "big." You shrink the psychological window: "You're not committing to forever. You're committing to not repeat the next 30 days."

Micro-commitments reduce flight response.

Compression Rule #4: Make delay feel like self-disrespect

Not shame—self-recognition:

"If you walk away now, you're not protecting yourself. You're protecting the problem."

This forces them to see "no" as loyalty to the problem, not logic.

Compression Rule #5: Strip away narrative and force a naked binary

"With everything you've admitted, are you choosing to fix it now or to keep living with it?"

Binary → Clarity.

Clarity → Decision.

> Boss Law #194: A binary question is
> the final compression tool, it forces
> identity to vote publicly.

IDENTITY TRAPS

Making "no" feel incompatible with who they believe they are. People do not buy because of information. They buy to maintain their identity.

If "no" threatens who they believe they are, they cannot choose it without psychological pain.

> Boss Law #195: You do not force decisions.
> You force identity to defend itself.

Identity Trap #1: Who they Said they are

You weaponise their own claims:

"You said you're done repeating this cycle, is that still true right now?"

If they say yes, "no" becomes hypocrisy. If they say no, they must admit they lied, aloud. Either outcome eliminates neutrality.

Identity Trap #2: Who they Cannot Tolerate Being

You reflect the version they refuse to become:

"The person you fear becoming is the one who keeps postponing the fix. Is that the path you're choosing?"

This makes inaction feel like self-betrayal, not delay.

Identity Trap #3: Who they Want to Become

You make yes the only path consistent with their desired identity:

"The future version of you doesn't hesitate—they act. Which version are you aligning with right now?"

They are not choosing your offer; they are choosing which self wins.

Identity Trap #4: Public Self Vs Private Self

Humans hate self-contradiction when spoken aloud:

"You came to this call because doing nothing is no longer acceptable. If you walk now, your actions are arguing against your own decision. Which do you trust—your words or your choices?"

You force them to choose one and live with the exposure.

Identity Trap #5: Status Cost

Not financial cost, identity cost:

"There is always a price. You either pay in money to fix it or pay in identity to stay the same. Which cost are you willing to live with?"

Now "no" has a price—ego, pride, dignity.

> Boss Law #196: When identity
> and decision collide, logic becomes irrelevant.
> Identity always wins.

IRREVERSIBILITY FRAMES

How to remove the possibility of retreat once they lean forward. Most prospects don't collapse at the beginning, they collapse after they feel the pull towards "yes." Irreversibility frames remove their ability to walk backwards without psychological damage.

> Boss Law #197: The moment someone
> leans forward, you must burn the bridge
> behind them.

Irreversibility Frame #1: The Turnback Cost

You make retreat feel expensive:

"Walking away now doesn't put you back to neutral—it puts you back with new proof that you avoided the fix again."

Retreat is now a declaration of fear, not a delay.

Irreversibility Frame #2: Expose the Interruption of Momentum

You don't let them believe they can "come back later" at the same state:

"If you break this momentum now, you won't return in the same state—you'll return with less confidence and more hesitation."

You tie delay to damage.

Irreversibility Frame #3: One-Way Door Logic

You remove the fantasy of a reversible decision:

"This is a one-way door—once you choose out, the problem stays in full control. There is no 'pause' outcome."

You collapse the illusion of neutrality.

Irreversibility Frame #4: Accountability Contrast

You show the identity contrast between the two futures:

"There are only two stories you can leave this call with, 'I fixed it today' or 'I avoided it again.' Which one do you live with?"

You force identity to vote publicly.

Irreversibility Frame #5: End of Escape Language

When they hesitate, you seal it clean:

"You've already revealed the truth and the cost. The only thing left is whether you act in alignment or break from your own logic."

You do not fight them, you make them fight themselves.

> Boss Law #198: Closing is not about pressure.
> It is about removing exits until action is
> the only self-consistent move.

INTERNAL RESISTANCE MAPPING

How to defeat the objection that they never speak aloud. The most dangerous objection is not the one they say, it's the one they protect silently. Verbal objections are tactical. Silent objections are identity-level.

> **Boss Law #199: People don't walk away because of price; they walk away because of unspoken fear.**

There are only three internal objections that ever exist under every "I need to think":

1. "I don't trust myself to follow through."
2. "If this fails, I prove I am the problem."
3. "Change threatens my current identity."

If you do not neutralise these, no external logic matters.

Internal Fear #1: "I don't trust myself"

This is the quiet root of 80% of hesitations. They aren't doubting you and their own execution.

You neutralise it by shifting responsibility from them to the system:

"You won't succeed because you feel ready, you'll succeed because the system removes drift and forces follow-through."

You make execution a function of structure, not self-belief.

Internal Fear #2: "If I try and fail, I prove I am the problem."

People avoid commitment not to avoid loss, but to avoid evidence.

You refract failure away from identity and onto method:

"If your current approach were capable of working, we wouldn't be having this conversation. Failure would be not upgrading the method / not trying the right one."

You protect their ego by redirecting blame to the old method.

Internal Fear #3: "Change threatens who I am today."
Humans subconsciously protect the identity they have built, even if it is miserable.

You destroy the illusion that stability = safety:

"Not changing is not preserving who you are. It is committing to become a more stuck version of yourself."

This reframes inaction as identity decay rather than protection.

THE META-MOVE: YOU BRING THE HIDDEN OBJECTION OUT WITHOUT ASKING FOR IT

You do not say: "What are you afraid of?"

That invites denial and ego defense. You name the fear for them before they voice it:

"Right now your head knows this is the right move, the only resistance left is the part of you that doesn't trust yourself to follow through. That is exactly why this exists."

When you name the hidden objection, they cannot hide behind it anymore.

Boss Law #200: The second an unspoken
fear is spoken aloud, it loses its power.

DECISION TRIGGER MECHANICS

How to force the mind to choose now instead of drifting. People do not struggle to decide because they lack information; they struggle because their brain have not been forced into a binary state.

A mind with three options will always drift.
A mind with two options will hesitate.
A mind with one survivable option will commit.

Boss Law #201: People don't decide when
they understand; they choose when
indecision becomes impossible.

Decision Triggers are phrases and structures that collapse all cognitive escape routes.

Trigger #1: Reducing the decision from identity → to moment

You shrink the weight of the choice:

"You're not deciding your future. You're deciding not to repeat the next 30 days."

You remove pressure without lowering commitment.

Trigger #2: Reversing the burden of proof

You make no require justification, not yes:

"Given everything you've admitted, the only thing that needs explaining is choosing to walk away—not choosing to fix it."

This flips the mental courtroom. Now no is on trial.

Trigger #3: Force a public internal vote

You require alignment with who they claimed to be:

"Are you acting like someone who is done with this or someone who is still negotiating with it?"

Not "do you want it?"/"who are you right now?" Identity obeys itself.

Trigger #4: Eliminate the "maybe" category

You remove the third lane entirely:

"There is no 'maybe' here—it's either we fix this now or you choose to live with it. Which path are you taking?"

No middle ground = no drift-state.

Trigger #5: Turn hesitation into exposure

You make indecision visible, not private:

"Hesitation right now is not confusion—it's the part of you that has kept you stuck trying to stay in control. Are you choosing that part or killing it?"

Once hesitation is seen, it dies.

**Boss Law #202: Drift survives in silence;
it dies when named and cornered.**

COMPLIANCE LOCK

How to make the "yes" irreversible in their mind before the transaction even happens. Most closes fail not because someone won't say yes, but because their yes is fragile and can be reversed by fear 30 seconds later.

A Boss does not just secure a yes; a Boss locks the yes into their identity before the card is ever out.

You lock compliance in three phases:

Phase 1. Future Self Confirmation

Immediately after they lean into yes, you anchor identity:

"Good, this is exactly what someone who is done with this chapter does."

You are no longer validating the decision; you are naming who they became by making it.

Phase 2. Public Declaration Frame

People honor decisions they declare:

"Before we process anything, I want you to say it clean: you are choosing to fix this now—correct?"

Once they speak it, reversal becomes psychologically expensive. Internal decisions are reversible. Spoken decisions are binding.

Phase 3. Chain-To-Path (Immediate micro-execution)

You do not let them float after yes. You force instant action to cement the identity.

Examples:
- Book the kickoff call while still on the line.

- Have them send their details immediately.
- Assign the first task before payment is entered.

This creates a sunk-cost anchor: "I already started—I am now the type who executes."

**Boss Law #204: Motion after yes is
the cement that prevents reversal.**

THE NO-BACKDOOR RULE

You never end a yes with:

- "Let me know if you change your mind"
- "Sleep on it if needed"
- "We'll reconnect tomorrow"

That reopens the escape door you spent 30 minutes sealing.

Instead, you end it with finality: "We start now."

Final. Neutral. Unquestioned.

WHY THIS WORKS

People do not stay loyal to decisions; they stay loyal to the identity they entered when they made them. The compliance lock ensures they cannot exit the decision without also leaving the identity they now publicly own.

**Boss Law #205: You don't protect the yes,
you make the cost of reversing it unbearable.**

THE IRREVERSIBLE CLOSE

A single seamless sequence that removes every exit before, during, and after the decision. This is the full psychological close, not a script but the logic stack in the correct order. When executed in sequence, "no" ceases to be a defensible option.

STEP 1: REMOVE ESCAPE PATHS BEFORE THE OFFER

You eliminate all alternative realities:

"If doing nothing worked, you wouldn't be here. Cheaper has already failed. DIY stalled you. The only real fork left is: fix it now or keep the problem."

(No pitch yet—only reality.)

STEP 2: FORCE THEM TO ADMIT THE COST OF NOT MOVING

"Another 90 days like this means another $_____ lost and the same life repeated. You already said that's not acceptable."

Now "no" = agreeing to a future they condemned themselves to.

STEP 3: COLLAPSE TIME

"There is no smarter month than this one. Nothing arriving later increases readiness—delay only compounds loss."

"Later" is now exposed as a lie.

STEP 4: IDENTITY TRAP

"A person who is actually done with this doesn't delay—they act. Are you that person or the person who repeats the cycle?"

They are choosing identity, not offer.

STEP 5: PRESCRIBE, NOT PITCH

"Here is how we fix it—we replace the failing system with a proven structure, and we execute immediately."

No features. No justification. Just finality.

STEP 6: STATE THE INVESTMENT WITHOUT SHRINKING

"The investment is $1000."

Silent. No defense.

STEP 7: DECISION DEMAND (BINARY ONLY)

"We start now—card or invoice?"

No third lane.

STEP 8: COMPLIANCE LOCK

After yes: "Say it clearly—you're choosing to fix this now."

Identity binds decisions. Then you move them into immediate micro-execution (the first task, the first step, the first onboarding action).

> **Boss Law #206: The close is not when they say yes, the close is when reversing yes would break their identity.**

Command delivery is not about charisma, persuasion, or pressure. It is about removing exits until the only psychologically coherent move is forward. You did not "sell" them. You made every alternative impossible.

OBJECTION ALCHEMY

How to turn resistance into compliance without chasing, convincing, or lowering your status. We enter this section with a core principle:

> **Boss Law #207: Objections are not barriers; they are escape attempts. Your job is not to answer them; your job is to remove the escape.**

Most people "handle" objections by explaining, defending, or negotiating.

A Boss does none of those.
A Boss converts the objection into a confession, leading back to the only logical conclusion: Move Now.

Objection Alchemy = You don't fight the objection. You redirect it back at the person who raised it until it collapses.

Before we touch specific objections, one foundational rule: You never answer an objection at face value. Once you answer a surface objection, you certify it as real. If you argue with their reason, you accept their frame—and you lose.

Objections are never what they say:

"Money" isn't money.
"Timing" isn't timing.
"Thinking" isn't thinking.

There is always a deeper driver underneath:

- Fear of commitment
- Fear of exposure
- Fear of failure
- Identity conflict
- Loss of control
- Ego preservation

Answering the words means you miss the cause.

THE 3-STEP OBJECTION ALCHEMY METHOD
Every objection, regardless of wording, is handled by the same sequence:

- STEP 1: NAME THE REAL SOURCE
- STEP 2: FORCE THEM TO OWN THE CONSEQUENCE OF RETREAT
- STEP 3: RETURN THEM TO THE BINARY DECISION

That is it. No debating. No teaching. No selling. Only the wording wrapper changes depending on the objection category.

THE ONLY 4 TYPES OF OBJECTIONS THAT EXIST

Despite hundreds of phrasings, every objection is one of these:

1. TIME OBJECTIONS: "Not now / I need to think / Maybe later"
2. MONEY OBJECTIONS: "Too expensive / Can't afford it / Need to wait for cash"
3. TRUST OBJECTIONS: "Not sure it will work / I've tried before / Need certainty"
4. CONTROL OBJECTIONS: "Let me check with ___ / I don't decide alone / I'm not ready to commit"

There are no others. If you handle the category, you handle every wording variation.

TIME OBJECTIONS

"I need to think" • "Not the right time" • "Maybe later" • "I'll revisit this soon"

We do NOT answer this with logic or patience. We convert it into a confession of avoidance.

Step 1: Name the Real Source (not what they said)

Time objections are never about time; they are about fear of acting now. You expose that gently or aggressively, depending on tone.

Cold surgical: "Thinking about it doesn't create new information—it just delays the decision you already know you need to make."

Dominant: "Thinking isn't the issue—committing is. This isn't a research problem, it's a courage problem."

Philosophical: "People don't delay because they need clarity—they delay because committing forces identity change."

All three make "time" indefensible.

Step 2: Force them to Own the Consequence of Retreat

You don't argue, you pin the cost back onto them: "If you leave this unchanged today, you're not preserving your situation—you're choosing to repeat it for another cycle. Is that a choice you're actually willing to own?"

Notice: You did not try to talk them into now; you made "later" an active, shameful decision.

Step 3: Return to Binary Decision

"So the plan is simple—fix it now or keep it as is. Which one are you choosing?"

Binary kills drift.

> **Boss Law #208: A time objection dies
> the moment "later" is exposed as a decision,
> not a delay.**

MONEY OBJECTIONS

"It's too expensive" • "I can't afford it" • "I need to save first" • "Maybe when money is better"

Money objections are never about money. If it were truly about money, they wouldn't be on the call—they'd be working, not evaluating. Money objections are about one of three deeper fears:

1. Fear of losing money without outcome (trust in system)
2. Fear that THEY won't execute (trust in self)
3. Fear of choosing now (money used as camouflage)

You never answer the money line. You convert it into a mirror of logic and consequence.

Step 1: Name the Real Source, Not the Words
Cold surgical: "If this was guaranteed to work, money wouldn't be the objection—so the objection isn't price, it's trust."

Dominant: "You've spent more money staying stuck than you will fixing it—this is not a cost issue, it's a comfort issue."

Philosophical: "Money objections are rarely about the fee—they're about the fear of making the wrong move and proving something about yourself."

You expose that money is a shield, not a barrier.

Step 2: Force them to Own the Cost of Not Paying
You do not defend the investment; you make "not investing" look more expensive.

"Not moving today is not free. It locks in the exact financial loss you said you can't continue. You are already paying, just with no upside."

You reframed "saving" as leaking.

Boss Law #209: Money is not the cost; stagnation is the cost. Money is the receipt.

Step 3: Return to the Binary

"So the choice isn't 'pay or not pay'. The choice is 'pay to fix it once' or 'keep paying in lost time, lost confidence, and lost income.' Which cost do you accept?"

Binary makes the illusion disappear.

Optional Final Snap (when they still cling)

Use only when they repeat the objection after reflection: "You already proved you can afford to stay stuck—the question is whether you can afford to stay stuck again."

That line exposes the self-betrayal of repeating the cycle.

TRUST OBJECTIONS

"What if it doesn't work?" • "I've been burned before." • "How do I know this is different?"

A trust objection is never about you, it is about their memory of a previous failure being projected forward. You do not defend your credibility. You do not try to reassure. You do not provide evidence like a salesman. You redirect the lens away from you and back onto reality.

Step 1: Name the Real Source

Cold surgical: "You don't doubt the method—you doubt repeating a disappointment."

Dominant: "You're not afraid this won't work—you're afraid to commit and find out you were the reason the last one didn't."

Philosophical: "People don't fear new decisions—they fear reliving old wounds."

You take the objection out of the "offer" and into the "past."

Step 2: Flip the Burden of Proof

You do not prove this will work. You make staying the same the bigger risk: "If you do nothing, you guarantee the very outcome you're afraid of: staying where you are."

Their fear now works against inaction, not against action.

Step 3: Differentiate this Decision from their Old One Without Defending

Not by saying "this is different because…"

That puts you on trial.

You shift the trial to their readiness, not your offer:

"The failure wasn't that you tried. It was that you tried without the structure, enforcement, and consequence you have now. This isn't a repeat unless you behave the same way."

Now the condition of success is them changing, not you proving.

Step 4: Return to Identity Binary

You pull them back to who they choose to be now:

"You either repeat the story where you protect yourself from risk and stay stuck, or you write the chapter where you act while still afraid. Which story do you choose to live with?"

No middle lane. No more theory.

Boss Law #210: Trust objections collapse
when staying the same becomes more
humiliating than risking change.

CONTROL OBJECTIONS

"I need to talk to my spouse/partner/mentor" • "I don't decide alone" •
"Let me check with someone first"

Control objections are not about permission, they are about
outsourcing responsibility so the decision cannot be blamed on them.
You do not attack the spouse or partner. You attack the psychology
of deferral.

Step 1: Name the Real Dynamic

Cold surgical: "You're not asking for input—you're asking for someone
else to carry the risk for you."

Dominant: "You want someone else to be responsible for the outcome so
you don't have to own it if it goes wrong."

Philosophical: "When people are unsure, they borrow someone else's
conviction so they don't have to test their own."

You expose the behavior, not the relationship.

Step 2: Reframe "Asking" As A Delay, Not A Requirement

"If you were certain this was the right move, you'd inform them, not ask
them. So the real issue isn't them, it's your hesitation."

This puts the spotlight back where it belongs: on them, not on the
3rd party.

Step 3: Collapse the Social Cover

You remove the usefulness of the external excuse: "Someone who is actually done with this problem doesn't outsource the decision to someone who's not living the consequence."

This destroys the legitimacy of deferral.

Step 4: Force them to Own it

"Just to be clear—if they said nothing and it was only your call, are you in or out?"

If they say IN → objection was fake → proceed to payment.

If they say OUT → they were using the other person as a shield → now it's exposed.

Step 5: Final Identity Snap (Use Only if they Still Hide)

"If you leave this call without committing, you're not protecting the relationship—you're protecting your hesitation and using them to do it. Is that the role you want to play?"

You didn't disrespect the spouse, you made the prospect confront the truth.

> Boss Law #211: Control objections are
> not about authority. They are about
> avoiding accountability. Remove the shield,
> the objection dies.

The Seamless Conversion Sequence. How to collapse ANY objection without debate and convert it back into a decision in one flow. At this stage, you have four categories of objections:

1. Time
2. Money
3. Trust
4. Control

But you do not run four different playbooks. You run one integrated response pattern that works on all of them.

THE 3-MOVE OBJECTION ALCHEMY SEQUENCE

Every objection, no matter the wording, is neutralised using this exact flow:

Move 1: Expose the Truth Behind the Objection

You never answer their words. You name the real engine beneath the words. Examples depending on tone:

- "That's not about timing — that's about hesitation."
- "That's not about price — that's about uncertainty."
- "That's not about them — that's about outsourcing responsibility."
- "That's not about the offer — that's about fear of failing again."

You do not fight what they said; you redefine it. This strips the objection of dignity.

> **Boss Law #212: Objections do not die when answered, they die when unmasked.**

Move 2: Force Them to Own the Cost of Retreat

You redirect the weight back onto the "no" path:

- "If you don't move now, you've already chosen to repeat the same outcome."

- "Doing nothing is not neutral, it is guaranteeing more of what you said you can't live with."
- "Refusing this path means you actively choose the one that is already failing."

You don't sell the "yes". You make "no" indefensible.

Move 3: Return to the Binary Decision

No debate. No negotiation. No third lane. You end the loop with a clean binary:

"So with everything you've admitted, do you choose to fix it now or to live with it?"

Binary forces a decision. Decision kills drift.

> Boss Law #213: Objections don't get solved,
> they get cornered until they collapse.

FULL INTEGRATED RESPONSE (ALL 3 MOVES APPLIED IN ONE FLOW)

Prospect: "I just need to think about it."

You: "Thinking isn't the issue, hesitation is. And hesitation is exactly what kept you stuck for months. If you walk away now, you're not preserving anything—you are repeating the exact outcome you said is unacceptable. So it's binary: fix it now or keep it. Which one are you choosing?"

No emotion. No selling. No defending. A Boss does not try to win the argument; a Boss removes every place the argument could hide.

Close of Integration Block

This section is now complete.

You now have:
- The structure of objections.
- The psychology beneath them.
- The universal kill-sequence.
- The integrated one-flow conversion pattern.

KILL SHOTS

The previous section taught you how to think. This now arms you with what to say. This is not theory. This is not persuasion philosophy. This is execution, word-for-word lines engineered to collapse objections in real time.

No rambling.
No debate.
No chasing.

You will not negotiate with hesitation; you will corner it. Use these lines exactly as written. A Boss does not convince. A Boss removes escape routes.

TIME OBJECTIONS: KILL SET

LEVEL 1. Controlled: "Thinking won't change anything, only deciding will."

LEVEL 2. Counter-attack: "If time solved this, it would already be improving. Delay is just repetition."

LEVEL 3. Ruthless Polished: "Postponing doesn't preserve your situation; it extends it. Fix it or repeat it, which one?"

If they Repeat it

"Days won't give clarity, only commitment does. So answer the real decision: fix now or live with it."

Amateur vs Boss

Amateur: "Sure, think about it and get back to me."

Boss: "Time changes nothing, decisions do. Fix or repeat?"

Enterprise-Grade Variant

"Waiting doesn't neutralise the loss, it compounds it. Indecision is already a decision. Correct now or extend the damage, which directive are you choosing?"

MONEY OBJECTIONS: KILL SET

LEVEL 1. Controlled: "You're not avoiding the investment, you're avoiding the decision."

LEVEL 2. Counter-attack: "Not fixing this is what's expensive—you're already paying for the problem every month."

LEVEL 3. Ruthless Polished: "You have two costs: pay once to solve it, or keep paying in lost time and income. Which cost do you choose?"

If They Repeat it

"Saying you can't afford it is the same as saying you can afford to stay stuck. Are you choosing that?"

Amateur vs Boss

Amateur: "I understand. Let me know when things improve."

Boss: "Money isn't the block, repeating this cycle is. Fix it or fund it again—decide."

Enterprise-Grade Variant

"Budget isn't the constraint, trajectory is. Every month you delay, the loss compounds. Correct now or extend the loss, what directive are we executing?"

TRUST OBJECTIONS: KILL SET

LEVEL 1. Controlled: "You're not doubting the solution, you're doubting a repeat of the past."

LEVEL 2. Counter-attack: "If doing nothing worked, you wouldn't still be here. Staying the same is the only guaranteed failure."

LEVEL 3. Ruthless Polished: "You either risk a new path, or you guarantee the old result. Safe or stuck—which do you choose?"

If they Repeat it

"You're not protecting yourself from failure, you're protecting the conditions that already failed you. Fix it or relive it?"

Amateur vs Boss

Amateur: "I get it. I hope you find something that works."

Boss: "This is not about the offer, it's about whether you repeat the same outcome again. Decide: new path or same cycle?"

Enterprise-Grade Variant

"The risk isn't in taking this step. The risk is in proving the old system again. You either change the mechanism or you validate the failure. What outcome are you willing to sign your name to?"

CONTROL OBJECTIONS: KILL SET

LEVEL 1. Controlled: "If you were certain, you would inform them—not ask them."

LEVEL 2. Counter-attack: "You want someone else to carry the responsibility so you don't have to own the outcome."

LEVEL 3. Ruthless Polished: "The person living the consequence is the one who must make the decision. Do you own it or outsource it?"

If they Repeat it

"If they gave no opinion at all, are you in or out? That is the real answer—not theirs."

Amateur vs Boss

Amateur: "Sure, talk to them and get back to me."

Boss: "You don't need their permission to stop losing. The decision is yours, choose ownership or delay."

Enterprise-Grade Variant

"External approval is a shield against responsibility. The choice still lands on you, proceed or perpetuate?"

You now hold the language that collapses hesitation, but a close is not complete when they say "yes." A close is complete when the yes becomes irreversible. Most sales are not lost before the decision; they are lost after the decision:

- buyer's remorse
- second-guessing
- external influence
- emotional recoil
- silence after the call

A Boss does not celebrate the "yes." A Boss stabilises the yes, so it cannot unwind. The following section exists for one purpose: To convert the decision into compliance and compliance into momentum before doubt returns.

You will not treat a new client like a signed contract, you will treat them like a freshly caught objection trying to escape. In the next section, you will build:

- A 24-hour post-close protocol.
- Psychological anchoring to prevent reversal.
- First-delivery moves that raise commitment instead of relaxing it.
- An onboarding structure that creates inevitability, not relief.

Because momentum is not born from agreement, momentum is born from immediate execution.

COMPLIANCE & ONBOARDING

The Moment After "Yes" Is When The Real Close Begins. Most amateurs relax after the yes. Bosses tighten control after the yes. A buyer who just said yes is not committed; they are chemically unstable:

- Adrenaline drops
- Doubt rises
- External opinions creep in
- Identity panic sets in ("Did I do the right thing?")

Your job in the first 24 hours is to remove all escape hatches before their nervous system tries to rescue them.

> Boss Law #214: A sale is not closed when they agree.
> It is closed when they can no longer retreat.

THE 24-HOUR LOCKDOWN PROTOCOL

Immediately after the yes, you execute three moves:

Move 1: Anchor the Decision with Identity

You don't validate their choice; you validate who they became by making it. "You didn't buy a program—you chose a different outcome than the one you were repeating."

You are not celebrating the transaction, you are reinforcing the new identity.

Move 2: Issue a Mandatory First Action Within 24 Hours

Not homework, a proof of commitment task.

Examples:
- Send a video introduction (forces them to show face)
- Fill a 3-question starter form (forces them to engage mentally)
- Book the kickoff call immediately (forces time investment)
- Upload a screenshot or file (forces participation)

The point is not the task, the point is to lock in behavioral momentum before doubt reactivates.

Move 3: Close All Escape Routes

You send a short, dominant confirmation message that frames the decision as final and irreversible.

Example: "We are now officially in motion. I'm treating this as an active engagement. Your first task is below and must be completed within the next 24 hours, so we begin from momentum, not hesitation."

No "let me know"
No "whenever you're ready"
No soft language.

You convert agreement into commitment.

Locking the Decision in Place (Identity + Irreversibility + First Win)

A "yes" is emotionally fragile until you do three things:

1. Anchor the identity they just stepped into.
2. Prevent psychological retreat.
3. Trigger a fast win so they feel momentum, not fear.

1. IDENTITY ANCHOR: Finalising Who They Became

You are not reminding them what they bought, you are reminding them who agreed to buy.

Gentle Version: "Today, you acted as the person who refuses to repeat old outcomes. That version of you is now in charge."

Neutral Version: "You made a non-reversible advancement decision. From this point, we operate from the upgraded identity—not the prior one."

Dominant Version: "You crossed a line today. The person who hesitates is no longer making your decisions—the one who executes is."

Identity anchoring removes space for second-guessing.

2. ANTI-REVERSAL FRAME: Kill Refund Logic Before It Surfaces

Before doubt appears, you define the decision as already irreversible.

Gentle: "We don't revisit decisions—we build on them."

Neutral: "This engagement is treated as active and in motion. The premise from here is forward, not reconsideration."

Dominant: "The window for indecision closed the moment you agreed. We're operating as committed, not reconsidering."

You do this before they ever try to walk backwards.

3. First Action = Proof of Commitment

The first action must be simple but undeniable. Not deep work, behavioral proof.

Examples:

- send a voice note introducing themselves
- complete a 3-question "starting point" form
- schedule kickoff call immediately
- upload before/after baseline photo (for fitness)
- send access credentials or files (B2B)

Then you frame it as mandatory, not optional:

Gentle: "Send this through within 24 hours so we begin with momentum."

Neutral: "This task must be completed in the next 24 hours to lock the engagement in."

Dominant: "You have 24 hours to submit this. No submission = Not serious. We don't start with words, we start with proof."

This converts an emotional yes into a behavioral yes; the second one is the real one.

ANTI-REMORSE & IRREVERSIBILITY

A "yes" is not safe until you remove the three forces that undo it:

1. Internal reversal (second-guessing)
2. External interference (spouse, friends, colleagues)
3. Structural reversibility (refunds, delays, soft starts)

This block kills all three upfront, briefly and decisively.

1. Psychological Anti-Remorse Frames

You speak before their fear speaks.

Gentle: "Doubt always shows up after big decisions—it's a signal you moved, not a sign you were wrong."

Neutral: "Second thoughts are a reflex of the old identity. We do not negotiate with the identity we just replaced."

Dominant: "Remorse is the voice of the version of you that kept you stuck. That voice is no longer in control."

2. Anti-Interference Shielding

You eliminate external influences BEFORE they arrive.

Gentle: "No one else lives the consequences of this choice—only you do, so only you get a vote."

Neutral: "Outside opinions are irrelevant because they do not carry the outcome—you do."

Dominant: "No third party gets a decision they don't personally pay for."

3. Structural Irreversibility (Contractual / Procedural)

You make the decision procedurally, not just emotionally. Rules you install:

- No "cooling off" window
- Immediate kickoff scheduling
- Delivery begins within 24–48 hours
- Refunds not positioned as safety but as forfeiture

Neutral contractual phrasing: "Engagement is active immediately. Work begins inside the first 48 hours. Once delivery initiates, reversal is no longer an option."

Dominant version: "Once we begin execution, the decision is not revisited. Momentum is enforced, not reconsidered."

4. Social Irreversibility (Public or Peer Commitment)

You use visibility to make backing out psychologically expensive.

Examples:
- Public or group announcement ("Welcome X, they just started…")
- Accountability partner assigned
- Shared dashboard or group channel entry
- Early "show your face" intro

Neutral framing: "You'll be introduced to the group once your first step is completed, which locks your commitment publicly."

Dominant framing: "You'll step into the arena in front of others executing, once you're seen there, backing out is not an option."

> Boss Law #215: A commitment becomes
> real when reversal would cost identity,
> not just money.

DELIVER, FAST-WIN, AND LOCK MOMENTUM (FIRST 72 HOURS)

Once the yes is stabilised, the objective shifts to:

1. Deliver something fast
2. Create an emotional "win hit"
3. Remove all friction to continued execution
4. Prevent the client from reverting to passive mode

You are not trying to impress them; you are trying to eliminate the possibility of regression.

1. The "Shock & Start" Delivery Principle

You do not wait for the perfect moment. You deliver something valuable and visible immediately.

Examples:
- First diagnostic/audit summary
- Personalised quick-start step
- Custom video
- Access link with structured next step
- Initial tactical correction (one improvement they can apply same-day)

Tone options:

Gentle: "Here is your first forward move—you begin today."

Neutral: "Execution starts immediately. Apply this before the next call."

Dominant: "No idle days. You begin now—here is the first step."

2. First Win Engineering (Psychological Hook)

You deliberately engineer an early, quick, visible, controllable win. Not a big result, a proof-of-progress hit.

Examples:
- Send five messages → get two replies
- Fix one offer line → instant clarity
- Change one CTA → immediate lead
- Upload one deck → team sees movement

The message is: "You did something—and it worked."

That moment is what binds them to continuation.

3. Micro-Commitment Chain (No Return to Idle Mode)

You do not allow them to finish the first task without assigning the next. After every action, you close with a new directive:

Gentle: "Once that's done, message me 'READY,' and I'll give you the next move."

Neutral: "Completion triggers the next directive—send proof once finished."

Dominant: "No gaps. When you finish this, send proof within the hour so I can issue the next instruction."

There is never a psychological "pause" zone.

4. Momentum Over Comfort

You are not there to make them feel safe; you are there to make them progress too far to retreat.

> **Boss Law #216: Clients don't stay because they pay. They remain because momentum makes quitting humiliating.**

RETENTION, UPSELL PRIMING & LIFETIME VALUE (SOP FORMAT)

Retention Architecture: Keep Clients From Slipping Backwards

Install these structural anchors immediately:

- Mandatory weekly checkpoint (written or voice)
- Zero-silent-days rule (no 72+ hr inactivity allowed)
- Standing recurring meeting or delivery cadence
- "Proof of progress" submission every week
- Escalation protocol if the client goes inactive (contact within 48h)

Retention trigger phrase to enforce compliance: "Progress is not optional—only the speed is."

CHECKPOINT

Weekly Structure:
- Check-in: 3 numbers / 1 issue / 1 commitment
- Correction: one targeted adjustment
- Command: next assignment with deadline

Monthly Structure:
- Gap review: where they lost momentum
- System update: refine operations, not goals
- Future lock: set next 30-day objective
- No idle states allowed between cycles

ANTI-DROPOUT SYSTEMS

Put these in place before they ever think of quitting:
- No "pause" options. Only "adapt and continue".
- If they fall behind. Reduce scope, not stop.
- Every inactive signal triggers a re-commitment call.
- If they hint at quitting. Reinforce identity frame, not retention pitch.

Standard enforcement line: "You don't exit because progress slowed—you exit only if the goal is achieved or replaced."

UPSELL PRIMING: WITHOUT SELLING

Do not pitch, architect inevitability.

Install these upstream:
- Future-state planning in every review call.
- Language that frames the current phase as "Phase 1".

- Show visible ceiling of current level to make the next level rational.
- Document their baseline and improvements to make ROI undeniable.

Clinical Upsell Bridge: "We are approaching the ceiling of Phase 1—the next growth sits in Phase 2. I'll map that for you when this current milestone is hit."

You are not asking, you are forecasting.

LIFETIME VALUE CONSTRUCTION

A client is not a transaction; it is a sequence. Your LTV model must include:

- Core offer → continuation offer → expansion offer.
- Scheduled renewal before the end of the term.
- Optional advisory, retainer, or alumni tier.
- Referral pipeline from satisfied clients.
- Partner / Affiliate layer for leveraged scale.

Clinical framing: "This engagement is designed as Stage 1 of an ongoing operating system—not a single event."

OPERATIONAL GOLDEN RULES

- Silence is an escalation trigger, not acceptance.
- Momentum is enforced, not negotiated.
- Renewal is pre-framed, not proposed.
- Upsell is a progression, not a pitch.
- Attrition is a system failure, not a client issue.

> Boss Law #217: Retention is not luck;
> it is engineered friction against regression.

The close is not when the money clears; it is when the new identity becomes irreversible.

You have now engineered:
- Stability of the decision
- Structure for compliance
- Systems for momentum
- Protection against reversal
- A path for retention and expansion

What began on Monday as an idea has become an infrastructure. This matters because: People do not rise to ambition, they fall to structure. Bosses build the structure that guarantees the rise. Now we transition to the final stage of this playbook, not to "end" the process, but to define what must never be undone. The conclusion is not a wrap-up; it is a transfer of responsibility from the pages to the reader's life. Momentum is now their duty. Not belief. Not hype. Not potential. Duty.

SALES FLOW MAP

PHASE 0: LEAD EMERGENCE

Executive Spine: A lead enters your world through digital or physical exposure.

Tactical:
- Sources: content, referral, DM reply, event conversation, handshake, intro from mutual contact, website form, QR code, live demo, workshop.
- The goal at this stage is not to sell, it is to convert awareness into conversation.
- Do not educate here. Do not pitch here. Do not send links. You only move them to conversation.

Branching Flags:

→ If online = move to DM open.
→ If in-person = move to micro-frame & transition to DM or call.

PHASE 1: CONVERT AWARENESS INTO CONVERSATION

Executive Spine: Turn a passive lead into an active dialogue.

Tactical:

- You initiate or respond with a problem-based opener, not a "let me know" or "thanks for following."
- Objective: extract a stated problem or desired outcome in their own words.
- This is the only necessary outcome of this phase—without a problem stated, no sale exists.

Examples of direction without pitch:

(Content environment) "What are you working on right now that you want to improve the fastest?"

(Event environment) "What's the one thing that's costing you the most right now?"

Branching Flags:

→ If they give a surface answer → probe once.
→ If they give a real pain or goal → advance to Qualification (Phase 2).
→ If they resist → exit or reposition (do not drag).

PHASE 2: QUALIFICATION & PATH DECISION

Executive Spine: Determine if they are a buyer, a browser, or a mismatch and route accordingly. You are not collecting information, you are classifying the lead into one of three lanes:

- HOT (Problem admitted + urgency + authority to decide)
- WARM (Problem admitted, but uncertainty/hesitation present)
- COLD (No problem ownership, only curiosity or social talk)

To classify, you extract three data points fast:

1. Problem Reality — Is this costing them something real?
2. Urgency — Are they trying to solve now or "sometime"?
3. Control — Are they the decision-maker or an influence layer only?

You do not need full context; you need a yes/no signal on all three.

Routing Rules from Qualification

If HOT → go straight to CALL (1-call close path).

If WARM → schedule a SHORT PRE-FRAME CALL first (2-call close path).

(Purpose: create certainty & authority before offering pricing)

If COLD → do NOT educate or nurture manually.

Move them to:
- low-effort broadcast nurture (content, email, group) OR
- exit the pipeline—do not carry dead weight

Branching Flags
→ HOT = skip prep / move to close environment immediately.
→ WARM = short preframe call → then close call later.
→ COLD = remove from active pipe.

PHASE 3: CALL → CLOSE SEQUENCE

Hot Leads → One-Call Close Path

Executive Spine:

<u>Qualify</u> → <u>Frame</u> → <u>Present</u> → <u>Collapse</u> → <u>Close</u> → <u>Lock</u>

Tactical Sequence:

1. Clarify Pain / Cost. Make them restate the consequence of not fixing it.
2. Future Frame. Articulate the alternative they want in concrete terms.
3. Authority Shift. You take control of the solution narrative.
4. Offer Presentation (Concise). 60-120 seconds max.
5. Immediate Objection Alchemy. Time/money/trust/control collapse.
6. Binary Close. "Fix now or repeat—which?".

Branching Flags:

If yes → go to Phase 5.

If stall → execute Kill Shot & re-binary.

If fake delay → treat as objection category, not time issue.

Warm Leads → Two-Call Close Path

CALL 1. PRE-FRAME CALL

Purpose: Eliminate uncertainty & convert "maybe later" into "we decide on next call."

Pre-frame Script Spine:
- "Here's the problem as you described it…"
- "Here is the cost of doing nothing…"
- "Here is the condition for solving it…"
- "On the second call, we will decide one direction—forward or not. Not a brainstorm."

Your only goal from Call 1 is to secure a locked decision commitment for Call 2.

CALL 2. COMMIT / CLOSE CALL

Same structure as the HOT lead one-call path, but shorter because the pre-frame already did the foundation work. Branch:

If yes → Phase 5.
If stall → objection collapse.
If delay request → treat as objection, not time.

In-Person

When closing face-to-face, the rules do not change, only the medium.

Executive Spine:

<u>Extract loss</u> → <u>Frame future</u> → <u>Command authority</u> → <u>Present concise</u> → <u>Collapse objection</u> → <u>Close binary</u>

Critical note: In person, you must transition them to written or scheduled follow-up immediately before they leave. Never end with verbal agreement alone.

PHASE 4: OBJECTION BRANCHING

At this phase, you are not "handling" objections; you are categorising and collapsing them. There are only four possible objection roots:

TIME / MONEY / TRUST / CONTROL

Everything said is just wording. You route immediately based on the root.

Objection Router

If they say:

"I need to think / not sure / maybe later" → TIME branch.

"I can't afford / too expensive / need to save" → MONEY branch.

"What if it doesn't work / I've been burned/need reassurance" → TRUST branch.

"I need to ask X / not my decision alone" → CONTROL branch.

You do not argue the sentence, you collapse the category using pre-written kill shots.

Branch Execution Rule

After you deploy one kill shot, you DO NOT EXPLAIN. You immediately return to a binary decision: "Fix or repeat—which are you choosing?"

If they present a second objection, you DO NOT run a new script.

You run the Objection Integration Law: "This is not about (new objection)—it's the same hesitation wearing a different sentence."

Then repeat binary.

Fail-Safe Branch (If they Still Resist After 2 Rounds)

You do not chase, you reposition: "You're not saying no to me—you're saying yes to the cost of staying the same. If that's your choice, own it clearly: are you choosing to remain where you are?"

If they accept that → they were never a buyer.

If they reject that → they close.

Boss Law #218: Objections don't block closes; weak boundaries do.

PHASE 5: YES → COMPLIANCE LOCK

A "yes" remains unstable until it is turned into behavior and becomes irreversible.

Immediate Anchoring (Identity, not Gratitude)

You do NOT say "thank you." You lock the identity behind the decision: "You just chose to stop repeating the old result—now we execute from that identity."

24-Hour Action Proof

You assign a task that requires movement, not thinking.

Examples:
- schedule next-step
- fill starter form
- send baseline video/file
- join platform/group
- send an intro voice note

Rule: The yes is not considered "real" until the task is completed.

Close All Exit Doors Up Front

You pre-frame irreversibility BEFORE remorse appears: "From this point we're in motion—we don't revisit the decision, only execute it."

Or a neutral variant if desired.

Social or Structural Lock

You add one or both.

Structural lock: Work begins within 24–48 hours = no refund logic possible.

Social lock: Public welcome / accountability message = retreat becomes embarrassing.

At the end of Phase 5, the buyer is no longer debating; they are executing.

PHASE 6: ONBOARDING & MOMENTUM

The purpose of onboarding is not orientation, it is preventing regression by forcing movement.

Zero-Idle Start

No waiting period. No, "we begin next week." You trigger execution immediately upon entry: "Your first action is below—complete it within the next 24 hours."

Engineer an Early Win

You deliver something that creates visible movement fast:
- One correction
- One breakthrough insight
- One fast-action step
- One measurable win

The goal is not progress, the goal is proof. Once they experience even a small win, retreat becomes psychologically expensive.

Micro-Commitment Chain

Every completed task immediately creates the next task.

No "empty space."

"Send DONE when finished and I'll give the next step."

Momentum is enforced, not optional.

Silence = Escalation

You do not allow clients to go dark. If 24–48 hours pass with no action, you escalate—you do NOT wait.

"Progress is mandatory—only the speed is negotiable. Report status."

No soft follow-ups. No babysitting. Compliance is part of the product.

PHASE 7: UPSELL PRIMING & LIFETIME VALUE ENTRY

The close is not the end of the relationship, it is the beginning of a value sequence. You do not "pitch later." You architect inevitability from the start.

Label Current Engagement as "Phase 1"

You condition the client from Day 1 that this is not the final level: "This is Phase 1—once we hit the ceiling of this phase, we move into Phase 2."

You do not ask them later, they assume continuation is part of the design.

Plant Future Milestones

You mention milestones that cannot be reached without the next tier: "Once we stabilize X, the next hurdle will be Y—and that is what we address in Phase 2."

You are not selling, you are forecasting.

Track Evidence that Makes Renewal Rational

You document:
- Baseline vs current state
- Tangible wins
- Avoided losses
- Remaining growth ceiling

People do not renew for hope, they renew for evidence plus unfinished upside.

Re-Decision Before Term Ends

You do not wait until the end of the engagement to discuss continuation. You re-close while results and momentum are active, not when they cool down.

"We are approaching the ceiling of Phase 1. The next step is locking Phase 2 before we hit that wall."

That is an upgrade, not a pitch.

SECTION SUMMARY

At the end of Phase 7, the client is:
- No longer reversible.
- Already mentally enrolled in the next commitment.
- Operating inside a system, not an experiment.
- Producing LTV instead of a one-time sale.

This completes the Sales Flow Map.

ENTERING THE SALES ASSETS SECTION

You now have the complete map, the architecture that moves a lead from first contact to irreversible commitment. A map, however, is not enough. Execution requires tools, instruments that remove guesswork and force consistency.

This section gives you those tools: checklists, flows, scripts, and metrics that can be used exactly as they are, without improvisation.

Purpose of this section: To convert the sales framework from a strategy you understand into a system you can execute every day without thinking.

These are not templates, these are operating assets. Use them exactly as written until closing becomes reflex.

ASSET #1: LEAD QUALIFICATION CHECKLIST

Purpose: To determine whether a lead is worth advancing to a call or needs to be filtered out without sounding interrogative or aggressive.

Use these questions (in DM, call, or in-person) until you have answers to all 6.

1. Current State

"Where are you right now with this—what's the reality?"

We are identifying the starting point.

2. Priority Level

"How important is it for you to change this right now on a scale of 1–10?"

We measure urgency from their own mouth.

3. Cost of Inaction

"What happens if nothing changes in the next 30–60 days?"

We establish consequence: No consequence = no sale.

4. Desired Outcome

"What would a win look like for you if this actually got solved?"

People buy futures, not features.

5. Previous Attempts

"What have you already tried, and what didn't work about it?"

This reveals trust objections before they surface later.

6. Decision Control

"When you do make decisions like this, do you usually decide solo or with someone else?"

This pre-identifies control objections.

Qualification Rule:

Advance only if at least 4 of these are true:
- They admitted a real problem.
- They rated urgency seven or above.
- They listed a real consequence.
- Their desired outcome is explicit.
- They have tried and failed before.
- They have decision authority or influence.

If fewer than four are true → do not advance. Move them to nurture or exit.

Boss Law #219: You don't close unqualified leads; you clean them out.

ASSET #2: SALES CALL PREP SHEET

Used before every call to prevent weak, improvised conversations. Purpose: A call should never begin with you "figuring things out as you go." This sheet forces clarity before the conversation starts, so you enter the call in control.

Prospect Snapshot

2–3 bullets only, not a bio.
- Problem they stated: _______________________________
- Consequence they admitted: _______________________________
- Desired outcome in their own words: _______________

If you cannot fill these in, the lead is not qualified. Return to DM and extract before scheduling the call.

Objection Anticipation

Check the most likely objection you expect from them:
- Time
- Money
- Trust
- Control

Pre-labeling removes surprise; objections are easy when expected.

Positioning Before Offer

Answer these for yourself before the call:

- What makes this problem urgent for them now—not later?

  ____

- What is the cost of not solving it in 30–60 days?

  ____

- What do you need them to admit out loud on the call before you present?

  ____

You do not present until urgency and cost are voiced by them, not you.

Call Objective (You Pick One)
- Book the commitment call (for 2-call path)
- Close on this call (for hot leads)
- Disqualify and exit (if mismatch)

A call with no declared objective becomes a conversation, not a close.

First Line & Last Line

Planned Open (first sentence you say):

____

Planned Binary Close (last sentence you will use):

____

You do not enter a call without knowing exactly how you will open and close.

Boss Law #220: A sales call fails before
it starts or succeeds before it begins,
based on preparation.

ASSET #3: DM → CALL → CLOSE SCRIPT FLOW

Hybrid system for online OR in-person leads transitioning into a close. This flow is not wordy, it is engineered to move a lead through phases without friction.

DM OPEN (Start a Real Conversation)

Goal: Extract the problem—not to sell.

"What are you trying to fix or improve right now that matters most?"

If they answer vaguely → "What specifically about that is not where you want it yet?"

You do not advance until a real problem is admitted.

Shift to Call (Without sounding needy)

Once there is a stated problem: "That's not a small issue. It's costing you. Easier to talk this through in 8–10 minutes than text it, can you do a quick call later today or tomorrow?"

If yes → schedule.

If stall → "If this is real enough to handle, it's real enough to talk for 10 minutes."

Pre-Frame Before Call Begins

You send this before the call so the frame is set: "On the call, we'll do three things:

1. Get total clarity on the problem.
2. Define the outcome you actually want.
3. Decide if you want to solve it now or not, no maybe.

They must agree to "decide" before you ever present.

Call Structure (Condensed Spine)

1. Clarify Pain — "Tell me what's actually happening right now."
2. Expose Cost — "What happens if this stays the same another 30–60 days?"
3. Define Future — "So the target you actually want is ________ correct?"
4. Authority Shift — "I know exactly why you're stuck. Here's the structure of the fix."
5. Offer (Brief) — "Here is how we solve it step by step…"
6. Binary Close — "Fix now or repeat — which path are you choosing?"

If Objection Appears

You do not argue the surface words. You route to the category (Time / Money / Trust / Control) and deploy a kill shot. Then return immediately to binary:

"So, correct it now or repeat it. Which one?"

No third lane.

Yes → Lock

If they say yes: "Good, we're in motion now. Step 1 is [task] within 24 hours. I'll send details now."

You do not end without a task and a deadline.

In-Person Adaptation (Same Flow, Different Entry)

If the lead comes from a real-world interaction:

1. Extract problem: "What's the biggest limitation for you right now?"
2. Transition to platform or call: "This is easier to unpack properly, I'll send you a link / let's schedule a quick call."
3. Resume the same sequence from Phase 2 onward. In-person only changes the medium, not the structure.

ASSET #4: FOLLOW-UP SEQUENCE

Purpose: Follow-up is not "checking in." Follow-up is re-entering control and forcing a decision window to reopen. There are only three scenarios you follow up on:

1. They ghosted after call.
2. They said "need time" / "later".
3. They soft-yes'd but didn't complete action.

Below are the exact follow-up lines for each—short, no warmth, no chasing.

Scenario 1. Ghost After Call

24–48 hours later: "Silence doesn't preserve your situation, it repeats it. Are you fixing this or keeping it? Reply with one word: NOW or LATER."

If still no reply after 48–72h: "No response = you've chosen to stay where you are. Before I close your file—confirm: are you intentionally choosing no change?"

If they stay silent → exit permanently.

Silence = disqualification, not a nurture lead.

Scenario 2. "I need time / I'll think about it"

Send 24–48 hours later: "Time doesn't change facts, only decisions do. Before I close this out: are you solving this now or repeating it?"

If they ask for more time again: "Repeated delay is a decision to stay the same. Own it if that's your choice—YES or NO?"

No third option is offered.

Scenario 3. They said YES, but didn't execute action

"A yes without action is a no in disguise. Are you moving forward or not? Decide now so we stop in limbo."

If they say "I will" but still don't act within 24h: "Understood—then this slot is released, and the file is closed. I don't hold space for hesitation."

If they re-enter later → they restart as a new lead, not a continuation.

Follow-Up Rules

- You never say "checking in," "just circling back," or anything soft.
- You never send more than two follow-ups—after that, they are not a buyer.
- You never nurture someone who has already rejected a decision.

Boss Law #221: Follow-up is not pursuit.
It is a final opportunity to choose
before you remove access.

ASSET #5: "IF THEY SAY X, YOU SAY Y" RESPONSE

No debate, no explaining, each line ends in control.

Time Objections

X: "I need to think about it."

Y: "Thinking doesn't add new information, only deciding does. Fix or repeat?"

X: "Maybe next month."

Y: "Delay duplicates the outcome you're trying to escape. Now or never?"

Money Objections

X: "I can't afford it."

Y: "Not fixing it is what's expensive. Pay once or keep paying in losses?"

X: "I need to save."

Y: "Saving keeps you stuck in the condition you said is unacceptable. Change or maintain?"

Trust Objections

X: "How do I know this will work?"

Y: "If doing nothing worked, we wouldn't be here. Risk new or repeat old?"

X: "I was burned before."

Y: "The burn came from staying with what failed, not from acting. Repeat or correct?"

Control Objections

X: "I need to talk to my spouse/partner."
Y: "If you were certain, you would inform them—not ask. Are you certain?"

X: "I don't make decisions alone."
Y: "No one else lives the consequence, only you do. Do you own this or not?"

Stalling / Escape Language

X: "Let me get back to you."
Y: "Silence won't change anything, only decisions do. Yes or no?"

X: "I'm not ready."
Y: "Not ready means you're choosing the current reality. Keep it or change it?"

Ghosting / Non-Replies

X: No response after conversation
Y: "No reply = repeat. Before I close this out, choose: NOW or LATER?"

Uncertainty

X: "I'm just not 100% sure."
Y: "Certainty comes after commitment—not before. Commit or restart the cycle?"

Boss Law #222: You don't wrestle with words;
you expose the decision beneath them.

ASSET #6: DAILY SALES RITUAL SHEET

A 10–20 minute non-negotiable daily routine to keep the pipeline alive and compounding. Purpose: Sales is not won in big moments; it is won in daily discipline. This ritual removes randomness and forces daily forward motion.

Daily Sales Ritual

1. PIPELINE REVIEW (1–2 min)
   - Check active leads
   - Identify 1–3 who need movement today

2. NEW OUTREACH (3–5 min)
   - Start 3–5 new conversations (DM or in-person if relevant)
   - Use problem openers, NOT pitches

3. FOLLOW-THROUGH (3–5 min)
   - Send the required follow-up to non-responders
   - Issue binary frames, not "check-ins"

4. ADVANCE HOT LEADS (3–5 min)
   - Push any active lead to call or decision
   - Remove anyone who is clearly not a buyer

5. SELF-PRIMING (1 min)
   - Read your closing binary for the day out loud

Rules of Daily Execution
- If you skip one day, momentum resets.
- If you do only the easy actions, the ritual does not count.
- The goal is not "more leads." The goal is movement through the pipeline.
- One decisive message is more valuable than 20 soft ones.

> Boss Law #223: Sales is not about volume.
> It is about daily non-negotiable movement.

ASSET #7: POST-CLOSE COMPLIANCE CHECKLIST
Used immediately after a "yes" to prevent reversal, delay, or collapse.

Purpose: A sale is not finished when they agree; it is finished when they cannot back out.

Post-Close Checklist: Run Immediately After "Yes"

1. Identity Anchor Delivered
   - "You didn't buy a program. You chose to end the repeated cycle."

2. Irreversibility Frame Stated
   - "We don't revisit decisions—we execute them."

3. First Action Assigned
   - Mandatory task within 24 hours (form, file, booking, intro video, etc.)

4. Deadline Stated Clearly
   - "This must be completed within 24 hours."

5. Confirmation Message Sent
   - Written message summarizing:
   - Engagement is active
   - First task
   - Deadline
   - No reconsideration language

6. Social/Structural Lock Applied (if relevant)
   - Group announcement/onboarding entry/kickoff scheduled.

7. File Status Updated
   - Lead removed from pipeline and moved to ACTIVE.

Fail-Safe Rules

- If the client does not complete the first task → you do not proceed to delivery.
- If they hesitate again → you re-frame, not re-sell.
- If they disappear → treat as unclosed and return to Objection Phase, not nurture.

Boss Law #224: A close without compliance is a delayed collapse.

ASSET #8: UPSELL TRIGGER & RENEWAL SCRIPT

Converts a satisfied client into a longer-term or higher-tier client without "pitching".

Purpose: Upsells are not sold; they are triggered when conditions are met.

When to Initiate an Upsell (Trigger Conditions)

You do not upsell randomly. You upsell when at least TWO of these are true:

- They achieved a visible win
- They are nearing the ceiling of the current level
- They expressed a desire for the next outcome
- They are compliant & responsive
- Their problem has evolved, not ended

If fewer than two are true → do not upsell yet.

How to Introduce the Next Level (No Pitch Language)

You do not "offer" the next phase; you frame it as the logical continuation.

Neutral framing: "We're approaching the end of what Phase 1 can produce. The next step is [NEXT PHASE FOCUS]. When you're ready, we can map that."

Authority framing: "The current system has taken you as far as it can. To continue advancing, we now shift into Phase 2."

The Actual Renewal / Upsale Close (Script)

Use once they signal openness: "Based on where you are now, the next 8–12 weeks would be focused on [X RESULT] using [Y METHOD]. If you want to proceed, we can lock Phase 2 now so there is no momentum gap. Yes or no?"

No pricing debate unless they confirm "yes."

If They Hesitate

"The only alternative to Phase 2 is slowing down or plateauing, and that is a regression in disguise. Continue or decline—which do you choose?"

FINAL RULE: Upsells are not sold; they are structurally inevitable.

BOSS SALES PLAYBOOK: TECHNICAL CLOSE

You now hold a complete sales operating system, not a set of phrases or tactics. From this point forward, the following are true:

- You know how to qualify leads before contact is wasted.
- You know how to move a conversation from message → call → decision.
- You know how to neutralise all four root objections without argument.
- You know how to enforce compliance after a yes.
- You know how to upsell without pitching.
- You know how to remove unqualified leads instead of nurturing them.

This is no longer about acquiring more knowledge. It is about repeating the system until the outcome stabilises. If this system is executed daily, sales become predictable. If it is not, nothing changes. This concludes the Boss Sales Playbook.

CONCLUSION
NO WAY BACK

You entered Day 1 with an identity that is no longer permitted to exist.

The story that justified your stagnation. The version of you that waited, hesitated, speculated, complained, or delayed was killed when you read the first chapter and kept going. Continuing past page one was the execution order; you crossed the threshold the moment you did not close the book.

Day 1 did not "teach" you anything. It destroyed the identity that held the previous you in place. Once you saw the mechanics of mediocrity, lies about time, readiness, money, and permission: You lost the ability to hide behind them without realising you were consciously choosing cowardice. That is irreversible. Awareness cannot be unlearned.

On Day 2, you became financially dangerous. Not because money appeared, but because value became weaponised. When you mapped your skill into a solution, you crossed the line from needing the world to being needed by it. That shift cannot be undone. Even if you never sell again, your brain now knows that money is not earned by worthiness; it is collected by solving problems. That realisation makes permanent victims impossible. There is no going back to "I don't know where to start". That sentence is now a fraud if spoken by you.

On Day 3, you eliminated the excuse of invisibility. You learned that obscurity was not fate, it was neglect. You built visibility not by begging for exposure but by inserting yourself into the streams where buyers already live. You now understand that attention is manufactured, not granted. That rewrites your future permanently. You can never again say "no one sees me" without knowing you chose not to be seen.

On Day 4, you crossed the most irreversible line: You learned how to convert. You saw that selling is not manipulation; it is leadership under pressure. You saw how objections reveal fear, not truth. You learned how decisions are forced, not found. Once you understand the mechanics of human decision-making, persuasion stops looking mystical. It becomes architecture. You cannot unknow the structure of commitment. You cannot pretend again that people "weren't ready." You will always know whether you failed because you were weak or because they were unqualified. That knowledge burns bridges behind you.

On Day 5, you eliminated the possibility of "one-time success." You learned that delivery is not fulfillment; it is asset creation. That upsells are not opportunistic, they are structural inevitabilities. That scale is not future, it is a process. You built the spine of a repeatable commercial system. This final shift is the death blow to your old life: You now know that income is not the result of opportunity; it is the result of systemised execution. You have crossed five irreversible thresholds—identity, value, visibility, sales, and continuity. There is no intellectual way back across them.

You did not finish this book with motivation; you finished it holding weapons.

The Boss Marketing Playbook removed the only universal excuse people cling to: "No one knows me." That is no longer available to you. You now possess the frameworks to create demand, not wait for it. To become present, persistent, and remembered without begging for relevance. That is not information, that is armament.

The Boss Sales Playbook removed the second and final excuse: "I don't know how to close." That excuse is now criminal to repeat. You were given the exact psychological architecture, objection routing, scripts, escalation paths, post-close compliance, and upsell inevitabilities. You are no longer in the category of the uncertain; you are in the category of the equipped.

Those two playbooks do three things at once:

1. They are weapons. You can attack the market on command.
2. They are certifications. You now operate at a level most don't understand.
3. They are obligation. Once armed, inaction becomes self-selected defeat.

From this point forward, your life is defined by only two states:

- You execute what you now know, and your outcomes realign accordingly.
- You refuse to execute, and you are no longer a victim, only a saboteur.

There is no third category. Not after this book. Not after these systems. Not after exposure to truth at this depth. You are not allowed to tell your story the same way again. You are not allowed to describe your life in the language of someone who didn't read this. You are not allowed to behave like someone who is still "figuring it out." You are not figuring. You are choosing.

You did not read a book; you eliminated your last defence. From here to the final page, there is one remaining act: Formalise the identity you are keeping, and legally abandon the one you are killing.

With the understanding that what you sign next is not a ritual, it is a burial and a contract in one. When you sign it, there is no re-entry to the version of you that existed before this week.

Only two futures remain: Execution or voluntary relapse.

Nothing else exists.

COMMAND PAGE

TERMINATION OF OLD SELF & ENACTMENT OF NEW STANDARD

By signing this document, I make the following declarations as final and binding:

1. The previous identity—including its habits, language, hesitation, and limitations—is terminated as of this signature. It will not be referenced, protected, or resurrected in any form.

2. From this moment forward, I operate under the Boss Standard, defined by execution over delay, decisions over doubt, and responsibility over excuse.

3. This decision is permanent. It will not be revisited, re-evaluated, or softened by time, mood, or circumstance.

CONSEQUENCE CLAUSE (NON-REVERSIBLE)

Failure to uphold this standard is a voluntary return to my old identity, a self-chosen act of sabotage, and a forfeiture of the right to complain about outcomes I refused to change.

There is no alternative interpretation and no third option.

PRINT NAME: _______________________________________

SIGNATURE: _______________________________________

DATE: _______________________________________

Boss Law #225: A new life is not earned
by wanting it, only by enforcing it.

100 BUSINESS IDEAS

1. Construction	2. Carpentry	3. Plumbing	4. Electrical
5. Painting	6. Landscaping	7. Roofing	8. Renovation / Repairs
9. Property Maintenance	10. Garden / Lawn Maintenance	11. Restaurant	12. Bar
13. Cafe	14. Nightclub	15. Food Truck	16. Catering
17. Meal Prep Services	18. Bakery	19. Juice Bar	20. Venue / Event Planning
21. Personal Trainer	22. Online Fitness Coaching	23. Sports Coaching	24. Mobile 1-on-1 Personalised Coaching
25. Sports Analyst	26. Yoga / Pilates / Gym Studio	27. Online Fitness Program	28. Nutritionist
29. Recovery Studio	30. Physiotherapist	31. Massage Therapist	32. Social Media Management
33. Content Creation	34. Branding Agency	35. Web Design	36. App Development
37. Digital Marketing Agency	38. Paid Ads Management	39. Email Marketing	40. IT Support
41. Graphic Design	42. Business / Sales Consulting	43. Performance / Leadership / Mindset Coaching	44. Appointment Setting / High Ticket Sales
45. Trader	46. Translator	47. Tutoring	48. Public Speaking
49. Affiliate Marketing	50. Online Courses	51. Education Platform	52. AI Implementation Services
53. Artwork	54. Buy, Fix & Resell	55. Buyer's Agent	56. Airbnb Hosting
57. Interior Designer	58. Architect	59. Tour Guide	60. Travel Agent
61. E-Commerce	62. Dropshipping Niche Store	63. Customised Apparel	64. Print on Demand
65. Beauty / Skincare / Oils Brand	66. Hair Products	67. Hairdresser / Barber	68. Perfume Private Labeling
69. Blogger	70. Twitch / Kick Streaming	71. Videography	72. Photographer
73. Podcast	74. YouTube Channel	75. Paid Newsletters	76. Mortgage Broker
77. Copywriting	78. Book / E-Book / Magazine	79. Singer / Songwriter	80. Performing Live
81. Talent Management	82. Subscription Boxes / Services	83. Personal Shopping	84. Delivery Driver
85. Mechanic	86. Jewelry	87. Vending Machine	88. DIY Cards
89. Dance School	90. Holiday / Event Decoration	91. Hand-Made Crafts	92. Furniture Assembly
93. Electronic Gadgets	94. House Cleaning / Housekeeping	95. Mobile Car Washing & Detailing	96. Pool / Window Cleaning
97. Pest Control	98. Pet Sitting / Grooming / Accessories	99. Membership Community	100. Brewing / Distilling

ABOUT THE AUTHOR

Alex Graorovski is a former semi-professional footballer who transitioned from an athlete into business by applying the same laws that shape elite performance: Discipline, repetition, precision, and execution under pressure. He did not abandon what competition had trained him in. He turned it into a business framework, building a football academy and operating by systems rather than chance.

He entered entrepreneurship without a safety net, connections, or inherited advantages. What replaced those was structure, the same structure documented in this book: Extract value, make it visible, convert with authority, deliver beyond expectation, and scale through process. His philosophy rejects the idea that success is based on personality or luck; it is operational.

This book is not written to inspire. It is written to eliminate the claim of "not knowing how." Once the mechanics are understood, the only remaining variable is whether a person chooses to execute or stay who they were.